The Literacy Leadership Handbook

The Literacy Leadership Handbook:

Best Practices for Developing Professional Literacy Communities

Cindy Lassonde

Kristine C. Tucker

PEARSON

Boston   Columbus   Indianapolis   New York   San Francisco   Upper Saddle River
Amsterdam   Cape Town   Dubai   London   Madrid   Milan   Munich   Paris   Montréal   Toronto
Delhi   Mexico City   São Paulo   Sydney   Hong Kong   Seoul   Singapore   Taipei   Tokyo

Vice President, Editor-in-Chief: Aurora Martínez Ramos
Associate Sponsoring Editor: Barbara Strickland
Editorial Assistant: Laura Marenghi
Marketing Manager: Krista Clark
Production Editor: Mary Beth Finch
Editorial Production Service: S4Carlisle Publishing Services
Manufacturing Buyer: Linda Sager
Electronic Composition: S4Carlisle Publishing Services
Cover Designer: Diane Lorenzo

Many of the designations by manufacturers and sellers to distinguish their products are claimed as trademarks. Where those designations appear in this book, and the publisher was aware of a trademark claim, the designations have been printed in initial caps or all caps.

Library of Congress Cataloging-in-Publication Data
Lassonde, Cindy.
 The literacy leadership handbook : best practices for developing professional literacy communities / Cindy Lassonde and Kristine C. Tucker.
  pages cm
 Includes index.
 ISBN-13: 978-0-13-301388-7
 ISBN-10: 0-13-301388-X
 1. Literacy—United States. 2. Reading—United States. 3. Literacy programs—United States.
4. Group reading—United States. 5. Educational leadership. I. Title.
 LC151.L33 2013
 302.2'244—dc23

                                                                                                2012049751

10

ISBN 10:   0-13-301388-X
ISBN 13: 978-0-13-301388-7

190018178

DEDICATIONS

To my mom...
who made me who I am
and loves me just for being me.
Thank you for always being there!

From Cindy

To my husband Eric...
Thank you for all you do in your quiet, humble, and loving way.
Thank you for the gift of both roots and wings so I can live authentically and creatively.
And thank you for being patient.
I love you.

To my sons, Bailey, Alex, and Mathew....
I love you. Always.

From Kristine

About the Authors

Cindy Lassonde is a professor in the Elementary Education and Reading Department at the State University of New York College at Oneonta, where she teaches undergraduate and graduate courses in literacy and special education. Formerly, she taught elementary language arts for over 20 years. As a writer, she is the author of numerous articles published in professional journals and has authored and edited 12 books on children's writing and literacy leadership. She is *most* proud of being the mom of three beautiful daughters and the wife of the love of her life!

Kristine C. Tucker is a seventh-grade language arts teacher at Central Middle School in Long Hill Township, New Jersey. Formerly, she taught in elementary education and special education. She has also served as a New Jersey state reading coach, K–12 literacy coach, and assistant professor of education. Her interests include literacy leadership and learning, experiential education, global education, humane education, and adult learning. Kristine is thankful for the love and support of her husband and three sons.

Contents

About the Contributors   xv

Foreword   xxi

Preface   xxiii

Acknowledgments   xxvi

Reframing the Culture of Literacy Leadership   2

Introduction   3

Literacy Leadership in Today's Educational and Political Forum   4

The Common Core State Standards Connection: The Call to Common Ground   TRACEY JOHNSON   6

Creating a Renaissance   7

Reframing Literacy Leadership   7

Evolving Roles and Approaches   8

   Individual Approach to Literacy Leadership   9

   Team Approach to Literacy Leadership   9

Response to Intervention (RTI) and the Literacy Leader:

It Definitely Takes a Team!   DAWN HAMLIN   11

Literacy Communities as Levers for Change   12

Professional Standards Supporting Literacy Leadership in Schools   13

Closing Thoughts   13

The Ethical Literacy Leader: Sharing the Responsibility for Literacy and Student Learning   JENNIFER IRELAND   14

     Cultivate Your Leadership Skills   15

Critical Voices: Complexities of Literacy Leadership
VIRGINIA GOATLEY   16

     Cultivate Your Leadership Skills   17

Questions for Reflection and Discussion 17

Practical Applications 18

    Classroom Activity 18

    Professional Development Activity 18

References 18

2 Portraying a Paradigm for Change 20

Introduction 21

Systems Thinking and Literacy Leadership 21

Response to Intervention (RTI) and the Literacy Leader: Moving Targets DAWN HAMLIN 22

Linking Systems Thinking to Purpose, Philosophy, and Pedagogy 23

The Common Core State Standards Connection: Navigating Implementation TRACEY JOHNSON 24

Narrative Inquiry, Experience, and Literacy Leadership 26

Appreciative Coaching and Literacy Leadership 32

Closing Thoughts 37

The Ethical Literacy Leader: The "A for Effort" Dilemma JILL LEWIS-SPECTOR 38

    Cultivate Your Leadership Skills 39

Critical Voices: Our Collaborative Journey of Change SANDRA ATHANS 40

    Cultivate Your Leadership Skills 41

Questions for Reflection and Discussion 42

Practical Applications 42

    Classroom Activity 42

    Professional Development Activity 42

References 42

3 Painting a Vision of Literacy Leadership   44

Introduction   45

Response to Intervention (RTI) and the Literacy Leader: Explicit and Intense: Welcome to the Emergency Room
DAWN HAMLIN   45

A Portrait of Goals for Literacy Leaders   45

Goal #1: Literacy Leaders Seek to Improve Evidence-Based Literacy Pedagogy   47

Goal #2: Literacy Leaders Seek to Improve the Performance of All Students   47

Goal #3: Literacy Leaders Seek to Affect School Culture   48

A Portrait of Effective Professional Development   49

Case Scenarios   49

The Common Core State Standards Connection: Continue to Press Toward the Mark   TRACEY JOHNSON   50

Painting a Portrait of Literacy-Learning Communities   54

Closing Thoughts   56

The Ethical Literacy Leader: Complementing Professional Standards with Personal Standards   DEBORAH BORDELON   57

Cultivate Your Leadership Skills   58

Critical Voices: Chipping Away at a Wall of Resistance
KATIE STOVER   58

Cultivate Your Leadership Skills   60

Questions for Reflection and Discussion   60

Practical Applications   61

Classroom Activity   61

Professional Development Activity   61

References   61

Nurturing a Mosaic of Adult Learners 64

Introduction 65

Working with a Mosaic of Adult Learners 65

The Common Core State Standards Connection: Preparing for the Journey Ahead TRACEY JOHNSON 66

Response to Intervention (RTI) and the Literacy Leader: Training for the Data Olympics DAWN HAMLIN 66

Assumption #1: Adult learners need to know why they are being asked to learn something new, before engaging in the learning process. 68

Assumption #2: Adult learners come to learning situations with a wealth of experience. 69

Assumption #3: Adults are ready to learn when they perceive the need to change to be more effective at what they do. 70

Assumption #4: Adults are motivated to learn after they experience the need for a change. 71

Assumption #5: Adults are motivated to learn based on internal needs. 74

Assumption #6: Adult learners are self-directing. 75

The Artist as Specialist 76

Closing Thoughts 77

The Ethical Literacy Leader: How Do I Keep on Working? MARY ANN LUCIANO 77

Cultivate Your Leadership Skills 79

Critical Voices: Maintaining Respectful Relationships—Or "You're Not the Boss of Me!" CAROLYN CHRYST 79

Cultivate Your Leadership Skills 80

Questions for Reflection and Discussion 80

Practical Applications 81

Classroom Activity 81

Professional Development Activity 81

References 81

5 Sketching Critical and Collaborative Communication   82

Introduction   83

Artful Communication   83

Etching Proactive Communication   85

Critical Communication   85

The Common Core State Standards Connection: In All Thy Getting . . . Get an Understanding   TRACEY JOHNSON   86

Collaborative Communication   88

Etching the Communication Process   89

The Speaker's Message   89

The Listener and the Response   92

Etching Literacy Contexts   94

Large-Group Discussions   94

Working with Small Groups or Individuals   95

Dealing with Confrontation and Negotiation   96

Communicating Through Writing   96

Response to Intervention (RTI) and the Literacy Leader: Decision Making and Reviewing   DAWN HAMLIN   97

Closing Thoughts   98

The Ethical Literacy Leader: Crafting Ethical Communication   JANET RICHARDS   98

Cultivate Your Leadership Skills   99

Critical Voices: Delivering the Hard Message   DAWN WENZEL   100

Cultivate Your Leadership Skills   101

Questions for Reflection and Discussion   102

Practical Applications   102

Classroom Activity   102

Professional Development Activity   102

References   103

6 Innovating a Mosaic of Creative Change 104

Introduction 105

Response to Intervention (RTI) and the Literacy Leader: Tools of the Trade DAWN HAMLIN 106

Creativity and Literacy Leadership 107

The Common Core State Standards Connection: Involvement and Influence in Planning Change TRACEY JOHNSON 109

Imagination, Creativity, and Innovation in Action at Ridge and Valley Charter School 110

Closing Thoughts 115

The Ethical Literacy Leader: Advocating for a Model of Equity SHERRY DISMUKE AND ROBIN SLY 116

Cultivate Your Leadership Skills 117

Critical Voices: Encouraging Teachers to Embrace Connectedness KATHLEEN MUIR 117

Cultivate Your Leadership Skills 120

Questions for Reflection and Discussion 120

Practical Applications 121

Classroom Activity 121

Professional Development Activity 121

References 121

7 Texturing with Resources 122

Introduction 123

The Texture of Professional Literacy Associations 123

The Texture of Online Professional Development and Networking 125

Response to Intervention (RTI) and the Literacy Leader: What's Up Online DAWN HAMLIN 125

The Common Core State Standards Connection: Built-In
Resources   TRACEY JOHNSON   126

The Texture of Partnerships   131

Building Caring Mentorship Relationships   131

Building Collaborative PD Models   132

The Ethical Literacy Leader: Travelling the Narrow Path
KYLE PACE   133

Cultivate Your Leadership Skills   134

Critical Voices: Collaborating with Stakeholders
SHELLY TERRELL   135

Cultivate Your Leadership Skills   136

Closing Thoughts   136

Questions for Reflection and Discussion   136

Practical Applications   137

Classroom Activity   137

Professional Development Activity   137

References   137

8 Celebrating the Masterpiece   138

Introduction   139

Assessing Progress   139

Collaborative, Team Leadership   140

Translating Values into Action   140

Resetting Goals   141

The Common Core State Standards Connection: Continue to Press
Toward the Mark   TRACEY JOHNSON   141

Celebrating Successes   142

Response to Intervention (RTI) and the Literacy Leader: Celebrating
Achievements   DAWN HAMLIN   143

Redefining Our Role and Job Description   144

Closing Thoughts   144

The Ethical Literacy Leader: Celebrating Successes Through "Star Tattoos" JANET RICHARDS 145

 Cultivate Your Leadership Skills 146

Critical Voices: Supporting Literacy Leadership KRISLYNN DENGLER 147

 Cultivate Your Leadership Skills 148

Questions for Reflection and Discussion 148

Practical Applications 149

 Classroom Activity 149

 Professional Development Activity 149

References 149

Appendix:

Literacy Professional Associations 151

American Reading Company by Jane Hileman 151

American Reading Forum by Nance Wilson and Michael French 153

Association of Literacy Educators and Researchers by Mary Roe, John Smith, and Rob Erwin 154

International Reading Association by Victoria Risko 155

Literacy Research Association by Patricia Anders 157

National Council of Teachers of English by Yvonne Siu-Runyan 158

Afterword 161

Index 163

Photo Credits 165

About the Contributors

Patricia Anders is a distinguished professor at the University of Arizona in the Language, Reading and Culture program. She is past president of the Literacy Research Association. Her scholarship, teaching, and service revolve around teacher education, community literacy, and workplace literacy.

Sandra Athans is National Board certified in Literacy: Reading—Language Arts. She is also the author of three books about reading comprehension and student motivation. Presently, she is a fourth-grade classroom teacher in the Chittenango Central school district, located in central New York, and also teaches graduate-level students as an adjunct professor at LeMoyne College in Syracuse.

Deborah Bordelon currently serves as the dean of the College of Education and dean of Graduate Studies at Governors State University in Illinois. She was also the co-chair for the International Reading Association's Professional Standards and Ethics Committee for 2011–2012. Her research interests and expertise include literacy education, quality teacher preparation at the traditional and alternative levels, recruitment of teachers in special education, under-represented populations in gifted education, and multiple intelligences.

Carolyn Chryst is an assistant professor in the Division of Education at the State University of New York College at Oneonta. She has a PhD in educational psychology, MEd in foundations of education, and BA in theater arts. She has worked with adult learners as a supervisor, coach, and mentor for more than 25 years in both formal and informal educational environments.

Krislynn Dengler is currently a lecturer in the Division of Education at the State University of New York College at Oneonta, where she primarily teaches methods-level courses. She formerly served as a high school principal at a rural, upstate New York public school. She is pursuing her doctorate at Binghamton University in educational theory and practice. She currently serves as chair-elect for the Reading and English Language Arts Special Interest Group for the Association of Teacher Educators.

Sherry Dismuke is a classroom teacher who has served as the cochair of her school's Response to Intervention (RTI) committee. She is pursuing a doctorate at Boise State University in curriculum and instruction with a focus on literacy and school improvement. Sherry teaches literacy classes and supervises teacher candidates for Boise State University. She presents nationally on issues related to RTI and underachieving students.

Kasey Errico has devoted her career to working with children as both a formal and informal educator. She started her career working with troubled adolescents and helped children and families develop strengths-based, family-centered plans in an effort to keep children in their home communities. Currently, she is a teacher/ guide at the Ridge and Valley Charter School in Blairstown, New Jersey. She is in her sixth year of teaching a sixth- to eithth-grade group in a primarily integrated, project-focused teaching environment. She is passionate about literacy and endeavors to be a model of life-long learning for her students.

Rob Erwin is associate professor in the Department of Professional Studies within the College of Education at Niagara University, coordinating the graduate literacy degree program. He has taught elementary school, worked in reading clinics, and served as university department chair, National Council for Accreditation of Teacher Education (NCATE) coordinator, and school consultant. He currently serves as president-elect of the Association of Literacy Educators and Researchers.

Michael French is professor and director of graduate education at Lourdes University. A former K–12 reading specialist in Minnesota and Wisconsin, his specialty in literacy is in the area of neurolinguistics and learning differences. Before Lourdes University, he served on the faculty at University of Wisconsin–Madison, Kansas State University, and Bowling Green State University. He has served on the editorial board of *The Reading Teacher* and is current editor-in-chief of the *American Reading Forum (ARF) Yearbook*.

Virginia Goatley is the director of research for the International Reading Association and a faculty member at the University at Albany. She has been involved in numerous research grants targeting elementary classroom literacy instruction. These projects included extensive collaboration with teachers, students, and teacher educators to use research as the basis for conversations in professional learning communities.

Dawn Hamlin is currently assistant professor at the State University of New York College at Oneonta. She helped develop the graduate program in special education, and is a past president of the New York State Council for Exceptional Children. She is a former special education teacher who taught in both traditional public schools and residential facilities.

Jane Hileman is a literacy activist, author of *The 100 Book Challenge*®, and chief executive officer of the American Reading Company™. Jane worked as a staff developer and reading specialist in the school district of Philadelphia and taught at the Graduate School of Education at the University of Pennsylvania. She has served as associate director of Philadelphia READS and on the National

Assessment of Educational Progress 2007 steering committee because of her field-work in reading assessment.

Jennifer Ireland is a National Board–certified Language Arts and Reading Teacher currently teaching at Lakeridge Middle School, Sumner school district, in Washington State. In addition to teaching, she serves as an instructional team leader, facilitating collaboration among members of the eighth-grade language arts department. She also serves as building learning coordinator, working with both building and district administrators, focusing on advancing the professional learning communities, and increasing student learning. Jennifer has also worked as a consultant with Penn State University, piloting and writing extension lessons for a Nonfiction Structure Strategy curriculum.

Dana Jackson is currently a master's student in the Language and Literacy program at Harvard Graduate School of Education. Her experience spans 14 years of service to public education at both the middle school and high school levels. She spent two of those years as a high school literacy coach in central New Jersey.

Tracey Johnson, whose career in education spans over 22 years, currently works at the New York State Education Department. She has coordinated the New York State Comprehensive Literacy Team, served as the New York State Education Department liaison for the Staff/Curriculum Development Network (S/CDN) and the New York State Council of Educational Associations (NYSCEA), and served as the secretary for the Professional Standards and Practices Board for Teaching. Tracey's diverse experiences include serving as a literacy coordinator at the Capital Region Board of Cooperative Educational Services (BOCES), an adjunct professor at Sage Graduate School in Troy, New York, and an ELA Coordinator/Reading First Coach in a charter school. Tracey coauthored a chapter in Peter Johnston's book *Reading to Learn: Lessons from Exemplary Fourth-Grade Teachers*.

Jill Lewis-Spector is vice president of the International Reading Association (IRA) and has served on its board of directors (2004–2007), as president of the IRA's LEADER Special Interest Group, and as chair of the IRA Governmental Relations Committee. She is a professor of literacy education at New Jersey City University. Jill has authored textbooks and multiple journal articles on advocacy, teacher education, and adolescent literacy, and has been an international volunteer for school-based literacy projects.

Mary Ann Luciano is director of the Catskill Regional Teacher Center. Her work as a literacy leader includes showcasing teachers who are literacy leaders. She has supported teacher action research on literacy; professional development sessions provided by teachers and others; conferences that have highlighted best practices and literacy teaching and learning; funding for school libraries for nonfiction books, poetry, and e-readers; and professional book-study groups.

Lisa Masi is a founding teacher/guide of the Ridge and Valley Charter School, a public charter school located in Blairstown, New Jersey, focused on earth literacy and experiential education. She is presently guiding students through their second of a two-year kindergarten/first-grade loop. Lisa is a member of the collaborative leadership team that guides the school in an administrative capacity. She recently earned a master's degree in Educating for Sustainability.

Kathleen Muir is currently the K–12 literacy coach at Cotee River Elementary School in Pasco County, Florida. Kathleen has presented at several conferences, including the Florida Reading Association, Florida Association for Supervision and Curriculum Development, and the Florida Council for the Social Studies. Her areas of interest include content literacy and transdisciplinary curriculum.

Kyle Pace is a K–12 instructional technology specialist and Google-certified teacher from Kansas City, Missouri. A former elementary school teacher, Kyle now provides instructional technology professional development to teachers across the district for which he currently works. Kyle also presents at conferences around the country on the impact of technology and social media in education. Follow Kyle on Twitter at http://twitter.com/kylepace. Kyle's website and blog can be found at http://www.kylepace.com.

Traci Pannullo is a founding trustee, curriculum coordinator, and member of the leadership team for Ridge and Valley Charter School, a groundbreaking public elementary school dedicated to education for a hopeful sustainable future. She is passionate about innovative, holistic, and progressive education that fosters humans' natural joy and propensity for learning. For the past 24 years, she has pursued the study and practice of alternative philosophies, such as Montessori, Waldorf, and democratic education, incorporating some of these ideas into her practice in teaching positions in traditional elementary settings. She holds a New Jersey supervisor certificate and a Master of Arts in Science as an Elementary Science Specialist, and is always looking for the larger context.

Janet Richards is a professor of literacy and research at the University of South Florida. She initiated and supervises field-based courses at a local community center, where she mentors her graduate students in a Community of Practice model. In this caring structure, doctoral and master's students learn to become literacy leaders. Many of Janet's publications focus on her field work.

Victoria J. Risko is a past president of the International Reading Association (2011–2012) and professor emerita, Vanderbilt University. She is a member of the Hall of Fame, International Reading Association. She is a former classroom teacher and reading specialist, and for years has collaborated with classroom teachers and curriculum specialists to provide literacy instruction that makes a difference for students, especially students who experience reading difficulties.

Mary Roe is currently a professor at Arizona State University, where she works with pre- and in-service teachers and conducts research linked to literacy learning and teacher education. Prior to this position, she was at Washington State University, University of Oregon, and University of Delaware. She spent 15 years in public education, initially as a middle-level English and Latin teacher, and then as a reading specialist.

Yvonne Siu-Runyan is past president of the National Council of Teachers of English. She is also professor emerita, University of Northern Colorado. Yvonne has taught grades K–12 (inclusive), and was a district reading specialist and language arts coordinator. She won the academic achievement award, the research award, and the outstanding teaching award presented by the University of Northern Colorado. She has 40-plus years of experience in the field.

Robin Sly is the 2009 Idaho State Teacher of the Year whose platform is the education of Twice-Exceptional students. Robin is a classroom teacher who is currently serving as the chairperson of her school's RTI committee. She has a master's degree in Literacy from Boise State University and is endorsed in gifted and talented education.

John Smith is a professor in and chair of the Department of Curriculum & Instruction at the University of Texas at Arlington. He has 10 years of elementary classroom teaching experience and 20 years of experience teaching at the university level. He served as reading coordinator for the Chapel Hill, North Carolina, school district, during which time the district's Chapter 1 program was recognized by the U.S. Department of Education as an exemplary program. He currently serves as president of the Association of Literacy Educators and Researchers.

Katie Stover is an assistant professor of education at Furman University in Greenville, South Carolina. Her research interests include translating research and theory into classroom practice, critical literacy, writing instruction, and teacher education. She has published in journals such as *The Reading Teacher* and the *Middle School Journal*.

Linda Sullivan is an elementary school teacher for the Newton, New Jersey, public school system. She has 15 years of teaching experience in both general and special education. Currently a third-grade classroom teacher, she has taken a lead role in literacy for the past six years. She has worked concurrently with district literacy coaches and has been a facilitator for the Newton, Andover, and Green townships' professional learning communities. Linda holds a master's degree in Educational Practices.

Shelly Sanchez Terrell is a teacher trainer, international speaker, and author of *The 30 Goals Challenge for Educators*. She has cofounded and organized the acclaimed educational projects Edchat and ELTChat, the Reform Symposium E-Conference, and the ELTON-nominated Virtual Round Table language and technology e-conference. Her prolific presence in the educator community through social media has been recognized by several notable entities, such as the *New York Times,* the *Washington Post, UNESCO Bangkok, Edweek,* and the United Federation of Teachers.

Dawn Wenzel, an elementary teacher, works as a network team specialist for the Norwich City school district. She also works with students and teachers in Grades K–5 as a classroom coach. Prior to working as a classroom coach, Dawn worked with students in her own classroom for seven years as a kindergarten and first-grade teacher. She is currently pursuing a certificate of advanced study in educational administration.

Nance S. Wilson is an associate professor and director of Middle Childhood Education at Lourdes University. A former middle school reading specialist, her specialty in literacy is in the areas of comprehension, metacognition, and negotiating narrative texts in the digital age. She is currently the chair of the American Reading Forum and has also served in numerous roles for this organization. In addition, she is the chair of the International Reading Association's (IRA) Middle School Reading Special Interest Group and the editor of *Reading in the Middle.* She has also served on the IRA's Children's and Young Adult Book Award Committee and other committees of the IRA.

Foreword

Richard L. Allington
Professor of Literacy Studies
University of Tennessee

I had just completed reading Pasi Sahlberg's *Finnish Lessons: What Can the World Learn from Educational Change in Finland?* (published by Teachers College Press) and then turned to *The Literacy Leadership Handbook: Best Practices for Developing Professional Literacy Communities* by Cindy Lassonde and Kristine Tucker. I mention this because Sahlberg describes how Finland developed a high-performing educational system. He notes that although Finland has little in the way of a national curriculum plan or accountability system, what was central to that achievement was teacher collaboration. Of course, it wasn't just teachers working together that created the Finnish educational success; but, as he writes, it seems unlikely the success could have been achieved without the hard collaborative work of Finnish teachers.

The United States has elected a very different framework to upgrade the quality of our schools and our educational outcomes. Framed by the top-down mandates delivered by federal and state education agencies and following the national guidelines embedded in legislative initiatives such as No Child Left Behind (NCLB), Response to Intervention (RTI), Race to the Top (RttT), and, most recently, the Common Core State Standards (CCSS), American teachers have spent the past decade just trying to keep up with all the required shifts and changes. We now know that the Reading First initiative of the NCLB brought many mandates for instructional change to elementary schools, but these mandated changes had little, if any, positive effects on student reading outcomes (Gamse, Jacob, Horst, Boulay, & Unlu, 2009). So Congress has terminated funding for that program but added several newer initiatives to the educational agenda.

American schools are now attempting to implement RTI, and in many states schools are trying to comply with the requirements of RttT and implement the CCSS. Whether outcomes will improve as a result of all this is the question. But because these efforts to reform American education do not greatly involve teachers in their development, I have my doubts as to whether any of these several efforts will produce much change in educational outcomes. My doubts are based on the lack of involvement of teachers in formulating the initiatives and in their implementation.

This is where *The Literacy Leadership Handbook* comes in. The model literacy leader developed in this book will foster collaboration among teachers as the primary strategy for improving the outcomes in a school (or school district). Central to this theme is working with adult learners. If we hope to improve teacher effectiveness, we must involve teachers as learners. That involvement comes more easily when we engage teachers in planning for their development.

This book provides clear guidelines for fostering such involvement and for fostering collaborative working environments where everyone becomes more expert every day. Lassonde and Tucker use examples from the work they have done with teachers and have included a number of first-person reports by both teachers and others working to improve education. All in all, this is a readable text, one that will often leave you wondering, "Why didn't I think of that?"

Following the advice that is offered in this book will support your efforts to become an effective literacy leader. You can't ask for a book to do much more.

Reference

Gamse, B. C., Jacob, R. T., Horst, M., Boulay, B., & Unlu, F. (2009). *Reading First impact study final report (NCEE 2009-4038)*. Washington, DC: National Center for Education Evaluation and Regional Assistance, Institute of Education Sciences, U.S. Department of Education.

Preface

Welcome to a new era of literacy leadership that is a result of a number of recent changes in education and the nation's economy. As you know, from the 1990s to the present day, there has been an upsurge in national and state policies related to literacy instruction, particularly reading instruction. From No Child Left Behind to Race to the Top, stakes for student performance as measured by test-based accountability have increased. States and school districts have felt the thumb of policy intervention on their backs and have reacted in various ways, from standards adoption to mandated curriculum compliance. Scientific research has become the driver of the reform and accountability movements. To top it off, the nation's economy has been slipping. Funding for education has decreased nationally, both within most states and for a majority of our local school districts. Administrators often have no choice but to cut back positions, services, programs, and materials and equipment.

As a result, the role of literacy leadership has been and is currently in the process of evolving, and in many contexts it is changing rapidly. Districts that used to have a literacy coach in each building—a position that was hailed as a powerful strategy for increasing students' literacy performance in the early 2000s—are now assigning one literacy coach or reading specialist to multiple schools. Job responsibilities are being combined as positions are cut. There is less support for classroom teachers and fewer positions that identify literacy leadership as their primary job description.

However, rather than provide fewer services to children, many educators are stepping up to the plate and taking on literacy-leadership roles themselves. Administrators, classroom teachers, staff, and community members are advocating for students' literacy needs in ways they may never have had to before. Collaboration among colleagues has sprouted to meet needs in a district. Technology has become a tool to disseminate information while saving money. Professional literacy communities are forming to provide support so that no educator or school district has to feel isolated. Educators who are speaking up and taking on these new leadership roles need our support and guidance to become agents of change in these days of education reform. That's what this book is all about.

The Literacy Leadership Handbook: Best Practices for Developing Professional Literacy Communities takes a proactive stance to help school districts' literacy leaders—whomever they may be—not only to see themselves as agents of change and growth, but also to facilitate their growth as professionals who promote growth in themselves, their colleagues, their students, the school culture, and the general profession. Each chapter integrates this theme of growth and development.

Anyone can be a literacy leader if they take it upon themselves to advocate for the development of a school culture that supports the democratic growth of knowledge, skills, and dispositions to escalate and motivate students' literacy learning. This book will help educators reach their goals as literacy advocates and leaders in their districts.

Literacy Leadership as an Art

Lucy Calkins's classic book *The Art of Teaching Writing* (1994) came to mind when we started writing this book. We see literacy leadership the way Calkins sees writing pedagogy—as an artful endeavor. It is philosophical, creative, and reflects an intrinsic and emergent process. Also, we see both writing and leadership as talents that can be cultivated, especially with the help of a good mentor. We know of highly effective, thoughtful literacy leaders. We also know others who try their best but don't possess the underlying artistic talent and the heart needed to feel and to be as effective as they possibly could be in the role. These observations are what lead us to make connections between the qualities and dispositions of an artist and those of a literacy leader.

Readers will notice right away that *The Literacy Leadership Handbook* follows an artistic metaphor. We selected the cover art because the mosaic tree reflects our vision of collaboration and growth among the literacy leaders of a school. Based on our vision of leadership as an artistic endeavor and talent, we have named and outlined each chapter with titles and headings that reflect art terms. We begin each chapter with a quote from an artist and an artistic image and have tied the quotes into the meaning of the chapters' content. We propose that after reading this book, readers will be able to paint a masterpiece of literacy leadership that reflects a democratic experience involving the collaboration of a literacy-learning community.

How to Use This Book

To best meet the needs of educators new to the field of literacy leadership, whether they are in college training programs right now and reading this book for a course or experienced teachers in the field who are taking on new leadership roles, we have chosen to integrate chapters demonstrating an overarching view of literacy leadership spotlighting multiple perspectives and the roles of numerous leaders within a system. Gone are the days when singular individuals—the principal, supervisor, or coach—led literacy learning. We must re-envision a system with literacy leadership valued as a shared and mutually enhancing responsibility—where learning is synergistic throughout the many niches of a school.

We recommend that this book be used within the context of a literacy-learning community so that the role of literacy leadership within a school building or district can be explored and discussed as groups of educators interact with the book. As ideas and issues arise, educators can discuss how their district envisions and negotiates the leadership roles and the literacy program. At the end of each chapter we have included Questions for Reflection and Discussion to spark conversations around the literacy portrait your school hopes to paint and a Practical Applications section that suggests ideas for applying the concepts in each chapter to classroom and professional development activities.

Another feature of this book is the incorporation of voices of practicing literacy leaders who are serving in schools across the nation. Each chapter exhibits features written by experts in the field that connect literacy leadership to the Common Core State Standards and Response to Intervention. In the Critical Voices and the Ethical Literacy Leader features in each chapter, educators speak honestly about personal issues and experiences they have had that relate to the chapter topics. Furthermore, Chapter 3 includes two interviews: the first with Linda Sullivan, elementary educator and literacy leader in Newton, New Jersey; the second with Dana Jackson, secondary educator and high school literacy coach in Franklin, New Jersey. In addition, Chapter 6 includes an interview with the literacy-leadership team at Ridge and Valley Charter School in Blairstown, New Jersey. Our contributors include classroom teachers across grade levels, literacy coaches and reading specialists working in school districts, representatives from outside agencies, teacher educators, administrators, and parents. We have reached out to colleagues from across the country and have represented both urban and rural school districts. See our About the Contributors pages for biographies of each contributor.

Welcome to the World of Literacy Leadership

You truly are one of a rare breed of people. You have chosen to become a school leader, a literacy leader. It is no easy job. It comes with many challenges and sometimes few accolades of recognition outside of knowing deep inside that you want the best for your students, your colleagues, and yourself. We are all learners and need to support and nurture each other.

We hope our book becomes an invaluable tool for you as you develop as a literacy leader. We would love to hear from you. Tell us what you're doing; share your triumphs and challenges. Let us know how we can help further. We don't have all of the answers, but with our combined experience in the field, we have strong networks upon which we can draw.

Be strong in your new role. Your colleagues and students are depending on you!

Cindy Lassonde
Cindy.Lassonde@oneonta.edu
Kristine Tucker
KTucker1972@yahoo.com

Reference

Calkins, L. M. (1994). *The art of teaching writing*. Portsmouth, NH: Heinemann.

Acknowledgments

We would like to thank all of our expert contributors for adding their voices and experiences to this book. This project has truly been a collaborative effort. Educators will benefit from reading your pieces. We are grateful to those who read and commented on earlier versions of the manuscript: Janice C. Brunson, Stafford County Public Schools; Carolyn Carlson, Washburn University; Nancy Hadaway, University of Texas at Arlington; James Johnston, Central Connecticut State University; Marie A. LaJenne, Western Oregon University; Priscilla Manarino-Leggett, Fayetteville State University; Barbara Mintzer, MacFarland Intermediate School; Barbara Pettegrew, Otterbein College; and Lora Raines, Georgia Military College and Sandersville Technical College.

Also, we would like to thank the professionals from Pearson who made this book possible, especially Aurora Martinez, Barbara Strickland, Tara Hartley, Michelle Hochberg, Mary Beth Finch, and Deepthi Mohankumar.

Our families also warrant our acknowledgment. Thanks to Mark for making Cindy tomato sandwiches so she could keep working on the computer a bit longer. Thanks to Kristine's family for understanding the necessity of stacks of books all over the house, concept maps covering the dining rooms walls and sliding glass door, and for eating out a lot so she could continue working at the dining room table.

And, finally, we want to thank our readers for picking up this book. Yours is a tough position to be in today. We acknowledge you for seeking new ideas, such as the methods and suggestions in this book, to tweak or transform your school's literacy work. We wish you the best as you engage creative change.

The Literacy Leadership Handbook

Reframing the Culture
of Literacy Leadership

> 66 *The greater danger for most of us lies not in setting our aim too high and falling short; but in setting our aim too low, and achieving our mark.* 99
>
> —MICHELANGELO

....
Introduction

W e'd like to begin our journey with you, our reader, by sharing the following experience that occurred recently between one of the authors, Kristine, and her nine-year-old son, Mathew. As you read their story, think about how Mathew and Michelangelo—in the chapter-opening quote—may have been inspired by narratives.

Thursday night, snug in bed, my son Mathew and I read the last line of Kate DiCamillo's (2006) book *The Miraculous Journey of Edward Tulane:* "Once, oh marvelous once, there was a rabbit who found his way home" (p. 200). Still wrapped within the emotions of the story, I held Mathew close as he cried softly, claiming how this was the saddest book he had ever read. Mathew talked about Edward's journey, commenting on all of the important plot points, how he felt about each, and how he'd like to create an adventure story of his own. All the while, I listened with full intention and presence. I was filled with awe and wonder witnessing my son as emotionally connected, inspired, artistic, empowered, and open to change and transformation.

Pulling back to experience the full wonder of literacy leadership, we can see how Mathew is both a learner and literacy leader. And so is Kristine. Together, they are thriving in an environment where literacy learning and literacy leadership are intimately connected. In this space, learning and leadership are experienced as truly synergistic, moment by moment. Here, learning and leadership are synonymous with developing as an agent of change. Mathew shows us he is learner, leader, and agent of change by actively tapping into his personal preferences and then intentionally choosing to read *The Miraculous Journey of Edward Tulane;* by deciding, consciously or not, how to engage with the text, paying close attention to plot and resonating emotionally with the characters; and by planning his own next steps as a reader and writer. We see Mathew learning from the text, leading his own literacy development, and ultimately growing (changing) as a human being. What we may not see, but do instinctively understand and value, is that Mathew is, in fact, changing the whole of his literacy environment and directing the next steps for Kristine as a literacy learner, leader, and agent of change!

What about Kristine? How is she a learner and literacy leader? In this exchange, we saw Kristine learning from Mathew as she focused her attention—watching and listening—to what he could do in this powerful literacy moment. We saw Kristine as a literacy leader in the way she was gently organizing, nurturing, and sustaining the literacy environment. She was also a responsible leader in the way she quietly celebrated Mathew's in-the-moment achievement. What we may not see, but do instinctively understand and value, is that Kristine is also changing the whole of the literacy environment! She is responsible for her own learning so Mathew can grow and achieve. She is accountable as a literacy leader by creating and re-creating the literacy environment for Mathew to thrive as a human being. She is working as an agent of change. Transformation is always happening here! This is literacy leadership.

The opening quote by Michelangelo inspires us to aim high in our lives! We are encouraged to create a bold mission and vision for education that will challenge us to change, grow, and transform. Within this bold mission and vision, literacy leaders have the potential, when inspired, to create vibrant schools where leaders, educators, and students grow, change, and transform all the time. When we declare that the purpose of education is for personal and social transformation, so too is literacy learning and literacy leadership. And that is what this book is all about! Let's read on to understand why education, literacy leadership, and learning must be transformative, especially within the context of today's educational and political milieu.

Literacy Leadership in Today's Educational and Political Forum

As classroom teachers, coaches, supervisors, and administrators, we are inundated with policies and practices to implement in the name of student achievement, career and college readiness, the market economy, and global competition. While we tend to enjoy linear cause-and-effect relationships, and cause-and-effect problem solving, the issues we face in education today cannot be drilled down to any one factor or central cause to fix. The world is far too complex for any quick fix. Education is far too complex. Schools are far too complex. Life in the classroom is far too complex!

What we can do, though, is set our sight on accepting and valuing the necessity of change in our lives. Change means growth and development. The natural world, humans, and all the other species among us are hard-wired for evolution! We are meant to change, grow, and develop to flourish and thrive within the systems that make up our lives. When we internalize this, we are ready to begin our work as leaders who create and re-create social institutions—schools—that are capable of educating students in ways that truly demonstrate academic excellence, personal growth, and social change. In setting this as our high aim, the next authentic move is to take stock of current reality.

Let's begin taking stock of our current reality in education. We need to consider how current shifts, policies, and practices influence literacy leadership.

- No Child Left Behind has influenced literacy leadership in a number of ways. School districts have restructured literacy leadership roles, placing professional development front and center. The expectations for assessment and accountability have increased for all students, across all schools. Leaders are pragmatically working together in demanding situations to exchange and supplement knowledge respectfully.

- Race to the Top influences literacy leadership, as it promotes objectives for rewarding teachers, focuses on teacher effectiveness, increases the number of effective leaders and teachers, and defines pathways for school leadership. These shifts spark the need for information and knowledge on topics such as how teachers learn, what teachers need to learn, and how to build capacity and sustainability regarding necessary changes in teacher learning.

- Common Core State Standards influence literacy leadership through new goals and standards regarding student performance and achievement. As a result, literacy leadership shifts to promote responsive changes in curriculum, instruction, and assessment. To further improve schools, literacy leaders will need to focus professional development efforts on learning the new standards and how to implement the standards through curriculum, instruction, and assessment. (See Tracey Johnson's Common Core State Standards Connection: The Call to Common Ground feature in this chapter.)

- Curriculum mapping influences literacy leadership, as it is considered part of the process of gap identification and analysis. Curriculum mapping is an "active" literacy-leadership process as educators work together to weave literacy across the curriculum. Many schools rely on committee work to collaboratively design these frameworks for curriculum mapping and integrating literacy across the content areas.

- Teacher evaluation reform influences literacy leadership in several ways. Literacy leaders inspire teachers to reflect and encourage a culture of ongoing professional development and learning that includes change and growth. Improving the effectiveness of teachers, however, does not necessarily come from the top. It comes from effective teaching and literacy leaders who foster and support it. As teaching performance and student achievement are systematically linked, the goals of teacher evaluation reform should focus on supporting professional learning, identifying teachers who need additional guidance and support—and perhaps a change of career—and recognizing expert teachers who can act as literacy leaders who contribute to the growth of effectiveness of their peers.

- Professional development influences literacy leadership as stakeholders assume responsibility for their own learning and the development of the school as a learning community. All school staff must play a part in improving school-wide professional development. All stakeholders must be involved in the planning, implementation, and assessment of professional learning.

- Student achievement and adequate yearly progress influence literacy leadership because students' literacy needs vary. Therefore, literacy programs must be district-designed to meet individual needs. School-based literacy leaders help immediately assess and address students' unique issues and

The Common Core State Standards Connection
The Call to Common Ground
—TRACEY JOHNSON

Tracey currently works at the New York State Education Department. Her diverse experiences include serving as literacy coordinator at the Capital Region Board of Cooperative Educational Services (BOCES), an adjunct professor at Sage Graduate School in Troy, New York, and an ELA Coordinator/Reading First Coach in a charter school.

Have you ever envisioned what learning is like through the lens of a child? What if the child once lived in a different region of the world or came from a different socioeconomic background? Oftentimes, our vision is impaired by our perceptions and biases, resulting from a tendency to focus on our differences; however, there is a need to find common ground.

The Common Core State Standards were developed on the foundation that, regardless of a child's zip code, there is a baseline of academic knowledge and skills that all students need in pursuit of colleges and careers. Forty-five states have adopted the Common Core State Standards for English Language Arts and History/Social Studies, Science, and Technical Subjects (National Governors Association Center for Best Practices, Council of Chief State School Officers, 2010). The adoption of these standards by the states establishes a call for common ground toward collaboration and cooperation on matters of public-education policy. These states, faced with student and teacher mobility, have alleviated these perceived barriers by already collaborating on common assessments, and modeling curricular and instructional materials. The Common Core State Standards articulate a move for common ground by emphasizing a shift toward a balance of literature and informational texts, a greater focus on text complexity, emphasis on argument and informative/explanatory writing, writing about sources or using evidence to inform argument, and a focus on formal and informal conversation and academic and domain-specific vocabulary.

The clarion call for common ground has gone out! Literacy leaders across the country (e.g., teachers, content experts, higher education faculty) have an opportunity to contribute to this transformational reform for the benefit of all students.

support teachers as they work collaboratively to provide a broad spectrum of context-specific literacies.

■ School, home, and community partnerships are integral to literacy leadership. Partnerships that develop personal relationships among school, home, and community leaders, who are also focused on improving students' learning, strengthen a school district. Literacy leaders can tap into homes and communities not only for valuable resources but to learn more about their students and how they learn. Within partnerships, literacy leaders will find opportunities for literacy to be used as a means of personal transformation and social change.

How are these shifts, policies, and practices influencing literacy leadership in your local context?

Although not easy, it is critical that we spend time within our school contexts in conversation with colleagues to understand how shifts, policies, and practices influence literacy leadership, and how literacy leadership, in turn, influences student learning, school culture, curriculum, assessment, professional development, communication practices, and norms for celebrating success. This kind of work is an entry point into systems thinking: one way of noticing how patterns of behavior influence what is deemed important in schools today. In applying systems thinking, we understand how cause-and-effect chains fail to capture the complexity of life in school. Instead, creating several causal loops or feedback cycles enables us to better understand how systems operate in our educational environments.

When we set our aim high to create schools designed for academic excellence, personal growth, and social transformation, we have identified a desired state: a mission or vision that is compelling, one that we are willing to bring into full life. When we acknowledge our current reality of how things actually are in a school—how shifts, policies, and practices influence literacy leadership—and how literacy leadership influences aspects of schooling that we deem important, we are naming where we are in relation to our stated mission and vision. This gap identification and analysis is where the deepest and perhaps most difficult work of literacy leadership is to be found and actualized—within the gap between vision and reality. But, within this gap, a renaissance can happen!

Creating a Renaissance

The word "renaissance" instantly brings forth images of change, growth, and development! Ravitch (2010) writes that the key to success of human development, and therefore human capital, is education. Whether our current educational system is mediocre or excellent, it will affect our economy and our lives—both civically and culturally—in the near and far future. Therefore, as literacy leaders we are challenged to create a "renaissance in education" (p. 224) that does more than simply exceed notions of a basic skills education. We are called to teach "the best of what has been thought and known and done" (p. 224) across disciplines. (Read how Jennifer Ireland's team worked toward transforming the culture of literacy leadership in The Ethical Literacy Leader feature at the end of this chapter.)

We agree that education needs a renaissance.

Reframing Literacy Leadership

Although the work to do is vast, literacy leadership is a path of hope, renewal, and promise. In this renaissance, literacy leadership is embodied as community cultural development, offering a rich canvas of ideology, mission, and vision. It is a framework of possibility and carries an ethos of liberation, transformation, and human and cultural development. It is a cultural container for educational philosophy, inspiration, artistry, and responsive pedagogy that is colorful, vibrant, dynamic, and diverse.

The culture we frame in this book is one that portrays literacy leadership as

- valuing traditional and alternative ways of knowing by blending artistry, intuition, and logic/reasoning;
- life-enhancing, purposeful, and authentic;
- democratic, antioppressive, and transformative, wherein all stakeholders' voices are valued and nurtured as learners and leaders; furthermore, multiple perspectives and diversity are sought, valued, and integral to growth and development;
- dialogic—privileging conversation as the catalyst for consciousness raising, personal transformation, and large-scale change; and
- integral to place- and community-based education, whereby teachers and students work and learn together as coinvestigators of relevant issues and concerns (Smith & Sobel, 2010).

Evolving Roles and Approaches

In this new renaissance of literacy leadership, what is needed most of all is a flattening of the hierarchy whereby all stakeholders embrace community-based learning. Although traditional roles may still exist, the difference lies in the way learning, leadership, communication, and knowledge are dispersed within the environment. Instead of *roles* coming together, *humans* come together to learn, dialogue, and create solutions within the context of literacy-leadership work. (Read Virginia Goatley's Critical Voices feature at the end of this chapter, in which she talks about the complexities of the evolving face of literacy leadership.)

We need to recognize the power and beauty of all stakeholders sharing in the leadership work of a literacy-learning community: students, community members, teachers, curriculum specialists, supervisors, department heads, vice-principals, principals, the superintendent, and members of the board of education. Transforming the toxic "us-against-them" mental model, this literacy-leadership renaissance is one of open dialogue and collaborative learning. Literacy leaders realize the power of blending individual, school, and community goals and objectives. Personal transformation is not lost to school and organizational transformation. Within this collaborative framework, literacy leaders

- engage in deep, continuous learning;
- contribute to ongoing, proactive, critical, and collaborative dialogue;

- participate in the development of curriculum, instruction, and assessment;
- create dynamic learning environments honoring the natural rhythm of learning, reflection, and renewal;
- apply appreciative leadership and coaching strategies to nurture and sustain growth, change, and development;
- collaboratively assess literacy learning and the literacy-leadership work; and
- celebrate success.

Individual Approach to Literacy Leadership

In some contexts, literacy leadership equates to what we call Lone-Ranger leadership, whereby one person is singularly responsible for championing academic achievement, designing and implementing professional development, furthering the literacy education agenda, and perhaps even whole-school reform. This role may be reserved for the principal or vice-principal, the literacy coach or reading specialist, or the curriculum coordinator or department supervisor. This paradigm often results in ineffective change due to an overemphasis on top-down management; micromanagement; loose, bottom-up, unfocused grassroots initiatives; or no real sign of leadership at all (Fullan, 2008). In addition, this model often privileges and perpetuates a dogmatic perspective on literacy education and leadership—one singular perspective, focus, and pedagogy.

Solo expeditions into literacy leadership are unsustainable for the individual charged with this responsibility and also unsustainable for the school as an organization. We can learn about effective leadership skills by looking to disciplines outside of education. For example, in *The Six Secrets of Change: What the Best Leaders Do to Help Their Organizations Survive and Thrive,* Michael Fullan writes, "A key reason why organizations do not sustain learning is that they focus on *individual* leaders. As individual leaders come and go, the company engages in episodic ups (if they are lucky) and downs" (Fullan, 2008, p. 107). The net effect is brain drain. When a talented, dynamic leader leaves, the acquired knowledge and change may leave, too. In this individual-as-leader approach, capacity is not built. Thus, for literacy leadership and change to stick, leadership must be distributed across a "flattened" system as shown in Figure 1.1. In this way, capacity is built through the diffusion of leadership, knowledge consumption and production, and even ownership-of-change processes.

Team Approach to Literacy Leadership

When literacy leadership is positioned and understood as a shared endeavor, possibilities open for a shift in school culture to take place. (Refer to this chapter's Response to Intervention [RTI] and the Literacy Leader feature to see what Dawn Hamlin suggests about working as a team to successfully implement RTI.) Literacy leadership needs to be cultivated throughout the entire school as a system

FIGURE 1.1   **(A) Individual Lone-Ranger Leadership; (B) A Flattened System of Diffused Leadership**

(A)

(B)

(Fullan, 2008). Literacy leaders work collaboratively to determine learning needs, allocate resources, experiment with pedagogical practices, plan and implement professional learning, reflect, conduct research, and so much more!

In addition, depending on the context, literacy leaders may find themselves working in a variety of capacities. Care should be taken as literacy leaders develop their talent and skill as consultants, coaches, mentors, facilitators, and supervisors. Literacy leaders will wear many hats, but first and foremost, literacy leaders are learners too. Collaboratively, literacy leaders can design their own learning journeys. This team approach to literacy leadership truly honors the growth and development of people, schools, and communities.

Response to Intervention (RTI) and the Literacy Leader

It Definitely Takes a Team!

—DAWN HAMLIN

Dawn is a former special education teacher who taught in both traditional public schools and residential facilities. Currently, she is assistant professor in the educational psychology department at SUNY College at Oneonta.

To achieve great success, implementing RTI takes a well-run team, on which the literacy leader plays an integral role. This team should include the reading specialist or literacy coach, the special education and general education teachers, paraprofessionals, families, and, of course, the students themselves. This team may also include administrators. While many administrators in many districts may not typically be involved in the day-to-day implementation of RTI, other districts have very connected and active leadership steering the processes.

Successful interventions, data collection, and program planning cannot and should not be handled alone. To effectively implement RTI, literacy leaders, special educators, and paraprofessionals will have to identify key components of the process, such as who is responsible for certain steps, how roles will be assigned, and how reviews will be done. All stakeholders must be very careful to keep the focus on obtaining *relevant, meaningful* data that can be used to improve instruction and provide targeted interventions (Bushell & Baer, 1994; Heward, 2003). All of this takes a great deal of planning. Questions that need to be addressed by the team are the following:

1. What types of assessments will be used? What are the critical skills expected at this level? Do the assessments reflect those skills? How frequently will skills be measured? If curriculum-based measurement (CBM) is used, who will develop the CBM probes?

2. Who will be responsible for actually assessing the students? Can one team member do weekly CBMs while another team member is responsible for daily probes if delicate data are needed for instructional decision making?

3. What role can the student play in the data collection process? Many students are fascinated by data charts and often they are able to graph their own data. (Of course, student-graphed data should be compared to teacher data for reliability, but this is a wonderful skill that can potentially generalize to different settings.)

4. How will data be reviewed? How will instructional or intervention decisions be made? Who will review interventions for procedural fidelity and research supporting its use? Who will score the CBM materials and other assessment materials? Who will conduct item analyses so the team can deliver fine-tuned instruction?

Read Jennifer Ireland's The Ethical Literacy Leader feature at the end of this chapter for an example of how a team can effectively work together to reach common goals as it upholds its principles and values. You will see how all stakeholders benefit as ethical generative learning communities are created.

Team approaches to literacy leadership need to be envisioned as thriving, vibrant, and creative networks. Many leaders within an organization are responsible for literacy learning and therefore literacy leadership. In what ways might this network work as a lever for transformation?

Literacy Communities as Levers for Change

Within our reframed literacy learning community, we must question the way we think, learn, and work if we are to truly generate a "life-affirming system" (Marshall, 2006, p. xvi) that liberates the "goodness and genius of all children" (p. xvi). Reflect on how you would answer these questions about your school's system:

- Does the current design of our system unleash the goodness and genius of children and adults in this system—our literacy leaders?
- Does the current design invite and nurture the power and creative use of literacy learning as a means of obtaining high academic achievement?
- Are we privileging literacy as just the ability to read, write, and pass tests while marginalizing the way literacy can be used by children and adults to creatively transform relationships, build community, and work for social change?

These questions spark the beginning of a much deeper dialogue that is waiting to happen in education and our schools. Wheatley (2002) reminds us that "Large and successful change efforts start with conversations among friends" (p. 25). Transformation begins when way deep inside a system a handful of colleagues decide they cannot tolerate something anymore and want to work toward an ambitious dream.

When we initiate the kind of conversation in which we inquire into a topic, an idea, an issue, or a concern that we care deeply about, we begin the real work of becoming generative learning communities (Marshall, 2006) that

- understand and nurture learning across the system through interdependence, diversity, and innovation;
- value learning as deep, collaborative, continuous, creative, and inquiry-based; and
- embrace the notion that learning results in mind shaping, community shaping, and world shaping—the transformation of mental models as sustainable change.

A generative literacy community is a vibrant, thriving network within which literacy leaders collaborate to accomplish the hard work of learning and literacy leadership.

Professional Standards Supporting Literacy Leadership in Schools

As literacy leaders, we must reflect upon the ways in which our work is intentionally connected to and supported by professional standards. Within the United States, each state has its own body of professional standards for school personnel. In addition, professional associations offer guidelines, standards, and position statements as benchmarks for literacy leadership and literacy education.

In reviewing the Standards for Reading Professionals (International Reading Association, 2010), it is evident that literacy leaders are required to demonstrate proficiency in the foundational knowledge of reading and writing; curriculum and instruction, assessment and evaluation; understanding diversity; creating literate environments; and professional learning and leadership. Literacy leaders—including students, parents, teacher assistants, school staff, and community members—are to aim high in the creation of generative and sustainable literacy education, literacy leadership, and learning communities.

Literacy leaders are urged to explore the Standards for Reading Professionals (International Reading Association, 2010). In doing so, give special time and attention to reading and unpacking not only the standards but the *major assumptions* supporting and driving the standards. In thinking about these assumptions, embrace awe, wonder, and creative tension! Recognize and celebrate your creative engagement in the literacy leadership renaissance we deeply need.

Closing Thoughts

This chapter was a journey into the forays of literacy leadership as community development work. We explored key concepts in literacy leadership and evolving roles of literacy leaders, considered the essence of generative learning communities, and identified the ways in which professional standards support this important work. Inspired by the work of Stephanie Pace Marshall and Margaret Wheatley, we invite all literacy leaders to enter this deeper conversation and community of literacy-leadership work.

At this time, we invite you to hear the voices of literacy leaders in the field as you read and contemplate The Ethical Literacy Leader and Critical Voices features in this chapter. Following each feature are questions in the Cultivate Your

Leadership Skills section to prompt your thinking as you work toward reframing the culture of literacy leadership in your context. To read more about all of our contributors' backgrounds, see the About the Contributors section of this text.

The Ethical Literacy Leader

Sharing the Responsibility for Literacy and Student Learning

—JENNIFER IRELAND

Jennifer is a National Board–certified language arts and reading teacher currently teaching at Lakeridge Middle School, Sumner school district, in Washington State. She serves as the instructional team leader and also as the building learning coordinator, building professional learning communities to improve student learning.

Three years ago the district administration where I work gave a directive to increase reading and math scores by 10 percent as we continue to work toward our adequate yearly progress (AYP) goals. As leader of the district's eighth-grade interdisciplinary team, I facilitated meetings so my colleagues and I could develop a plan to address the needs of our students.

Our team comprises two teachers for each content area of science, math, and English as well as one special education teacher. As teachers and literacy leaders, our team believes we have an ethical responsibility to build literacy across the content areas to prepare students for their future academic, professional, and personal lives. We build our instructional goals on this strong ethical and philosophical foundation.

After much discussion and analysis of students' work and scores, we found we needed cross-curricular literacy integration and a system of identifying students who struggle with grade-level skills. We discovered our students learn most effectively when immersed in common language: vocabulary that has been identified for application in all content areas. We knew that common language would

deepen students' comprehension in the individual content areas and develop an understanding of how the disciplines overlap in the real world. Our team decided on common language and metacognitive process questions that could be used in all of our classrooms. We planned to use these common terms across the content areas: "infer," "explain," and "analyze." We composed specific reading process questions.

We focused our weekly team meetings on planning a structured process for students to receive additional instruction during a weekly 60-minute advisory time. Each content-area teacher brought a list of students who were identified, based on common classroom assessments, as needing further help on a skill. We sorted our students according to their needs. By working together, we were able to negotiate a focus for each session: math, science, or English. We made the groups small (15 students) and the rest of us took on larger groups for enrichment. Our administration was highly supportive of our restructuring of our advisory time and allowed us the opportunity to take this risk in reshuffling students each week.

After a semester of using common language and process questions, we found in our classroom discussions and in our students' work examples of our students talking about the similarities among our classrooms. Each of my colleagues was excited to come to our meetings to share the classroom data that they had gleaned from their common assessments. They brought student samples that generated new ideas of how we could work together to improve our students' learning. We discovered that the students were speaking in terms of literacy during class discussions and in their work, as well as reflecting on their own learning, and using similar methods in different classes to communicate their ideas. Further, we found that most of our students (about 70–80 percent) were successfully learning the skills after initial instruction based on common assessment data; about 15 percent needed moderate reteaching, and about 5–7 percent needed intensive instruction following a retake on the specific skill due to significant gaps in previous skills. We were able to catch the 15 percent at the moment they faced difficulty and provide an intervention.

The first year our team continued to meet, seeking further literacy connections. Each member of our team became a literacy leader, creating new lesson plans that integrated literacy concepts tailored to different content-area needs, and exploring natural connections and strategies to help students read and write in the content areas. We saw remarkable growth in these students, not only in our classrooms but also on the state tests that year. The number of our students meeting the standards in science went from 40 percent to 63 percent in two years, in reading from 61 percent to 69 percent, and in math from 49 percent to 52 percent. As a team we believed in our students' ability to succeed in their grade-level content classes by having the support and reteaching opportunity provided in the intervention classes. We are happy to report our ethical and philosophical goals provided a strong foundation on which to build a team-generated plan of instruction and intervention.

As a team, we continue to challenge ourselves and each other, and it is our commitment to student learning and collaboration that makes us all literacy leaders, going the distance and continuing to carve out time during our school day to analyze student data, analyze needs, and reteach. We continually ask ourselves if we are doing everything in our power to ensure the learning of our students. We must consistently evaluate our instruction and creatively address the needs of our students to ensure their learning, because it is their lives, their future, and their ability to become successful adults that are at stake. These are the values we must uphold as ethical literacy leaders.

Cultivate Your Leadership Skills

1. Ravitch (2010) proposes literacy leaders inspire a "renaissance in education" (p. 224). How is Jennifer's team working toward transforming the culture of literacy leadership?
2. How does Jennifer's interdisciplinary team meet the Standards for Reading Professionals (International Reading Association, 2010) outlined in this chapter?
3. How would this feature have been written if Jennifer had taken a Lone-Ranger approach to the administrator's directive to increase reading and math scores?

Critical Voices

Complexities of Literacy Leadership

—VIRGINIA GOATLEY

Virginia is currently serving as the director of research for the International Reading Association. As a faculty member at the University at Albany, she has been involved in extensive collaboration with teachers, students, and teacher educators to use research as the basis for conversations in professional learning communities.

In the midst of a video interview, my coworker recently asked me to share a story about someone who inspired me as an educator and who should be celebrated as a teacher. I thought about this for a bit and my answer surprised both of us. I said it was the children I met along the way, and then provided examples of my first-grade students from long ago, the fourth graders in a research study, my many nieces and nephews, and so forth. With each child, I learn new ways of teaching, facilitating, and creating contexts for success. So, it made sense to me that Chapter 1 starts with a vignette about Mathew as a reader and a writer. Teaching involves learning, and the children are at the heart of how we learn.

Literacy leadership revolves around the complex and integrated nature of teaching and learning. As noted in the chapter, literacy leadership involves many stakeholders and different definitions of what leadership should and could provide. We are in the midst of many changes creating a moment in time where leadership is critically needed. Policymakers are challenging teachers to provide evidence that they are highly effective. State guidelines require students to take high-stakes tests that have critical implications for their own learning environment and the evaluation of their teachers. Administrators, publishers, education departments, and the media are all providing guidelines for how literacy should be taught. In the end, literacy leaders need to be professionals who can make strategic decisions

about what instruction particular children will need to build on their successes and keep high expectations for what they will learn next.

Over time, I have been fortunate to collaborate with many literacy leaders who have been engaged in this complex dynamic of keeping a focus on student learning while navigating the policy, curriculum, instruction, and assessment demands placed upon them. Since the chapter so nicely defines literacy leadership and outlines related roles and responsibilities, it prompted me to consider my own experiences with literacy leaders. I offer some key characteristics of literacy leaders that help provide the framework for successful teaching:

■ Literacy leaders are professionals who inquire about their practice and are open to new ideas.

■ Literacy leaders take the challenge of improving their practice, rather the relying on the belief they already know all there is to know.

■ Literacy leaders build trusting relationships to create a system-wide community where learners are expected to be successful.

■ Literacy leaders take responsibility for creating a successful context for learning, rather than blaming others or excusing poor practice.

■ Literacy leaders provide professional development to others, but also assume they need to be participants in professional learning as well.

■ Literacy leaders are critical consumers of research who stay current with new studies and the implications for practice.

■ Literacy leaders are advocates for children and young adults, joining in the policy and instructional conversations to offer their voice in ongoing decision making about required practice.

As I wrote this list, I was thinking of the many teachers, administrators, teacher educators, researchers, and policymakers who are literacy leaders and whom I've met along my educational journey. But, as Chapter 1 encourages us to do, I could easily envision the students as literacy leaders as well, especially when they are given the opportunity to thrive in thoughtful, caring contexts for learning.

Cultivate Your Leadership Skills

1. Virginia provides a bulleted list of key characteristics of literacy leaders in this feature. How does this list connect with the definition of literacy leaders described in this chapter?

2. If literacy leaders may be teachers, administrators, students, and other stakeholders in the learning community, how might the list of key characteristics of literacy leaders in this feature be viewed or accomplished by the various leadership roles?

3. This chapter describes generative learning communities. How do the characteristics of these communities connect with Virginia's perspective of literacy leadership as developed in this feature?

Questions for Reflection and Discussion

1. How is your literacy-leadership work connected to and supported by professional state standards and standards generated by professional associations?

2. Reflect upon your school's mission and vision statements. To what degree do they reflect literacy leadership and sustainable learning for all stakeholders? How might you revise the mission and/or vision with literacy leadership and sustainable learning in mind? How will you fold the revised mission and vision statements into your daily work as a literacy leader?

3. Does open dialogue exist in your local context? If so, which stakeholders are included? Who is excluded? Whom will you invite to join the conversation? What are some potentially positive consequences of this shift in participation?

4. To what degree are place- and community-based education understood and used? Does this warrant further inquiry? To what degree is antioppressive education understood? Does this warrant further inquiry?

5. Coming full circle, reread Michelangelo's quote with which the chapter begins. Now that you've read and reflected on this chapter, in what ways do you see the quote connecting to the culture of literacy leadership?

Practical Applications

How might this chapter apply to your teaching context and experience? Try these activities:

Classroom Activity

Take time in September, and as the school year unfolds, to discover, advertise, and tap into the many ways students, their families, and the local community advance literacy leadership. Focusing on students, cocreate literacy-related interest and skill surveys to discover ways in which students view themselves as literacy leaders. Together, mine the data to discover student strengths regarding literacy leadership. With students, create Go-To posters illuminating which students excel in particular areas. Nurture student expertise by

modeling how students can turn to each other for literacy-leadership support across the school day. The use of surveys, data mining, and distributing expertise can be replicated in this same way regarding family and community literacy-leadership support.

Professional Development Activity

With a group of colleagues, envision the kind of learning community you need in order to thrive as a learner and leader. Share stories about the kind of learning community that currently exists where you work to understand the current reality. Find the gap and create a plan for how you will grow a thriving, vibrant community to meet your needs.

References

Bushell, D., Jr., & Baer, D. M. (1994). Measurably superior instruction means close, continual contact with the relevant outcome data. Revolutionary! In R. Gardner III, D. M. Sainato, J. O. Cooper, T. E. Heron, W. L. Heward, J. Eshleman, & T. A. Grossi (Eds.), *Behavior analysis in education: Focus on measurably superior instruction* (pp. 3–10). Pacific Grove, CA: Brooks/Cole.

DiCamillo, K. (2006). *The miraculous journey of Edward Tulane.* Cambridge, MA: Candlewick Press.

Fullan, M. (2008). *The six secrets of change: What the best leaders do to help their organizations survive and thrive.* San Francisco, CA: Jossey-Bass.

Heward, W. L. (2003). Ten faulty notions about teaching and learning that hinder the effectiveness of special education. *Journal of Special Education, 36*(4), 186–205.

International Reading Association. (2010). *Standards for reading professionals.* Newark, DE: Author.

Marshall, S. P. (2006). *The power to transform: Leadership that brings learning and schooling to life.* San Francisco, CA: Jossey-Bass.

National Governors Association Center for Best Practices, Council of Chief State School

Officers. (2010). *Common core state standards.* Washington, DC: Author.

Ravitch, D. (2010). *The death and life of the great American school system: How testing and choice are undermining education.* New York: Basic Books.

Smith, G.A., & Sobel, D. (2010). *Place-and community-based education in schools.* NewYork, NY: Routledge.

Wheatley, M. J. (2002). *Turning to one another: Simple conversations to restore hope to the future.* San Francisco, CA: Berrett-Koehler Publishers.

Portraying a Paradigm for Change

> ❝Great things are not done by impulse, but by a series of small things brought together.❞
>
> —VINCENT VAN GOGH

Introduction

When we think back to how we felt entering the field of education and literacy, or taking on a new teaching or leadership role within the field, we likely remember moving into the work with energy, passion, and enthusiasm. We remember how in those new beginnings we wanted to know it all, experience it all, and to accomplish it all in a time frame of having it all done . . . yesterday! We wanted to have everything figured out quickly, efficiently, and neatly.

Hopefully, with time spent in the profession, we have grown to acquire a bit of wisdom, learning that wanting to figure out the mystery of it all quickly is valiant, yet impulsive, and the momentum so incredibly difficult to sustain. We agree with Van Gogh. Change in the field of education, literacy leadership in particular, is actualized through a series of processes that creatively emerge and unfold over time. Yes, epiphanies do happen! And we love them for what they are—magnificent bursts of insight. Epiphanies are sudden and wonderful and life-altering. But, the change experience we need for literacy leadership is the kind that is deep, enduring, appreciative, and, above all, respectful.

Literacy leadership is surely a creative endeavor. We are responsible for helping people grow into their own mastery. Our work each day, moment by moment, is marked by how well we are helping others develop their minds, talents, and skills. This is deep work. And, when we seek out quick fixes, we negate our prime objective. An appropriate shift can be made by turning toward philosophy and practices that support our prime objective. Because our calling is deep and humane, literacy leaders need to work from a knowledge base that includes systems thinking, narrative inquiry, and appreciative coaching. This is our paradigm for change.

We turn our attention first to systems thinking. Read Dawn Hamlin's Response to Intervention feature in this chapter for an example of systems thinking and change.

Systems Thinking and Literacy Leadership

Understanding the nuances of literacy education is critical for the literacy leader, but just understanding them is not enough. To be an agent of social change through literacy leadership, we need to learn the nuances of systems thinking to create environments where change is healthy and sustainable. Systems thinking will propel us through the old paradigm of factory-style schooling into a more holistic, ecological, learner-centered, interdisciplinary, and responsive leadership paradigm.

Response to Intervention (RTI) and the Literacy Leader

Moving Targets

—DAWN HAMLIN

Dawn is currently assistant professor at SUNY College at Oneonta. She is a former special education teacher who taught in both traditional public schools and residential facilities.

The RTI movement began in the realm of special education well over a decade ago. It was a response to an ever-increasing population of students who were identified as learning disabled due to a significant discrepancy between their IQ and their achievement. Special education leaders, including Doug and Linda Fuchs among others, realized that something was not working within the traditional paradigm of special education evaluation, identification, and, potentially, general education instruction.

Too many students were not actually learning disabled; rather, they were curriculum and instructional "casualties." Poor curriculum or ineffective instruction made some students appear to be learning disabled. It appeared that a focus on evidence-based practices and earlier interventions was often missing from the traditional classroom and prereferral process. Decisions based on quality student data were also lacking. Too many minority populations were over-represented and girls were often under-represented.

Something had to change, and RTI is the result. This was and is a major systems change in the fields of both special and general education. We are still working on getting all stakeholders up to speed on the processes of RTI and how to implement it successfully. One of the hardest challenges has been to parcel out who is responsible for what within the differing tiers of the RTI model.

In spite of the many challenges involved in a major change like RTI, things are looking up. Recent years have seen the number of students across the United States identified as "learning disabled" plateau. Another positive outcome has been that minority over-representation has decreased in school districts where RTI was successfully implemented. Also, more girls who were overlooked are now being identified and receiving support (VanDerHeyden, Witt, & Gilbertson, 2007; VanDerHeyden, Witt, & Naquin, 2003).

Applying systems thinking, literacy leaders can influence the school environment by

■ advocating that schools are living systems that continually grow, learn, and change;

■ creating learning communities that resemble interconnected networks so information, communication, and collaboration are shared by all;

■ coaching others to use cycles and feedback loops so it is easy to see and understand how thinking and behavior influence goal setting, professional learning, communication patterns, collaboration, shared resources, assessment, and celebration;

- modeling a democratic respect for the sharing of power, voice, and responsibility; and

- promoting health and wellness of people as vital to the development of a healthy organization as a whole.

Using systems thinking, literacy leaders are able to see the whole of school as a learning community and its interrelated parts. With this knowledge base, we can influence school culture and learning for the better. We will be more prepared to help people change their thinking and behavior in ways that truly resonate with the spirit of a collaborative learning community. As we develop in our ability to apply systems thinking, our courage grows and literacy leaders will find themselves ready to engage colleagues in beneficial and complex conversations and learning.

Linking Systems Thinking to Purpose, Philosophy, and Pedagogy

As literacy leaders, it is important to talk with others about the purpose of schooling and education. Yes, our mission and vision statements are posted. It's likely for these statements to be easily read on our school websites and documents for the community. But, when was the last time we *really* checked in with our mission and vision statements? When was the last time we thought about their timeliness? Have we considered recently how these statements are the vital link to our literacy-leadership work? Do we see ourselves as learners and leaders in the wording?

Applying systems thinking to see wholeness and connection between purpose, philosophy, and pedagogy, literacy leaders can work for realignment. (Read this chapter's The Common Core State Standards feature by Tracey Johnson for ideas about how the new standards will help align instruction.) Through complex conversations and learning, literacy leaders can help people align their beliefs about the purpose of school and corresponding educational philosophy and practice. This work must be field based. Yes, it is true that we learned about this in our teacher education programs; but it is within our professional development programs that the link between thinking and behavior manifests and grows! Literacy leaders are responsible for the difficult work of nurturing the positive that already exists while helping others to assess the gap between their espoused theories and the current reality of school and classroom practice. Through realignment, we are helping people grow into their own mastery.

The Common Core State Standards Connection
Navigating Implementation
—TRACEY JOHNSON

Tracey's career in education spans over 22 years. She has taught at all educational levels, developed curriculum, provided professional development to persistently low-achieving schools, and mentored teachers. She is currently employed at the New York State Education Department.

The work of a literacy leader is multilayered, requiring perseverance and innovation (Allen, 2006). The role of a literacy leader is not always clearly defined as he or she moves throughout a district into unchartered territories supporting learning and change.

It is in this uncertainty that one has to be clear about what is non-negotiable. Are teachers providing students with opportunities to write creatively, drawing from personal experiences? Are teachers structuring opportunities for students to have conversations and develop arguments based on the texts they have read? Are teachers using prereading strategies to help all students fully understand a text through discussion and/or overviews of context, vocabulary, and the author's craft prior to reading? Are teachers creating learning experiences that build knowledge using informational texts, not just literature? Are teachers providing instruction in academic vocabulary to support students' understanding of complex texts?

The Common Core State Standards is the framework in which all other professional development decisions are made. These standards cross all instructional boundaries and require a clear pathway to be fully implemented effectively.

Nationally, teachers across grades K–12 are in the process of navigating the implementation of the Common Core State Standards. The literacy leader's role becomes less ambiguous as the leader engages teachers and administrators in the process of changing instruction and ensuring that these changes are visible.

From the district office to the parent-teacher conference, the literacy leader has to convey the message that . . . "in the end it will be teachers who make a difference in children's school lives. It is teachers who will either lead the change or resist and stymie it. The focus of school change has to be on supporting teachers in their efforts to become more expert and reorganizing all aspects of the educational system so that they can teach as they expertly know how" (Allington, cited in Allen, 2006, p. 46).

L. M. Zinn (2004), a leader in the field of adult learning, describes how beliefs, values, and worldview or philosophies, whether consciously or not, shape our thinking, the decisions we make, and our corresponding behavior. Oftentimes, what we think, say, and do are mismatched or contradictory! We go about our work believing that all is well. Yet, when we have the support to reflect on this alignment, we may realize there is a gap between our thinking, behavior, and the results we are trying to achieve.

Therefore, we all need to reflect on what we want, what we say we do, and what we are actually doing. It is important for literacy leaders to help others recognize that dissonance is a part of life in general and that it surely shows up within our schools and classrooms. But, we can work on this—and in doing so we will transform lives.

As literacy leaders, we can learn more about critical thinking and how to use it so we can check in on possible discrepancies between espoused theories, the results we want, and the current reality of our minds, talents, and skills. Doing so requires that we move into what may be perceived as uncomfortable or really difficult work. And it is! So, we tend to avoid it.

Literacy leaders are responsible for helping others grow in their ability to examine the discrepancies between beliefs, values, and philosophies and action taken within the school and classroom setting. Please remember that this is gap identification and analysis, *not* to be confused as a deficit framework. We are not looking to find problems. We are not focusing on the negative. What we are doing is helping people to grow in their ability to self-direct change in their own lives. Literacy leadership is about helping people see what is already working, checking in with the results we want, identifying and understanding any gap, and creating change to align our mission and vision, thinking, and behavior. A courageous, collaborative literacy community can do this!

Literacy leaders initiate this kind of work through collaboration and intentional conversation. Our strategy is to discover how purpose, philosophy, and effective literacy practices are at work in the school environment. Learning organizations are host to a variety of diverse beliefs about purpose, philosophy, and classroom practices. How do we figure out what is working?

Here again we apply systems thinking as integral to the dialogue we generate and nurture. Literacy leaders ask the following of themselves and others:

- What are we truly nurturing? Are we developing
    - ✓ intellectual, moral, spiritual, and aesthetic domains (*liberal education*);
    - ✓ skills and behavior change (*behavioral education*);
    - ✓ citizenship, democratic processes, and critical thinking skills (*progressive education*);
    - ✓ personal development and self-actualization (*humanistic education*); and
    - ✓ social change (*radical education*)?
- What is the purpose of education and literacy leadership within our school context?
    - ✓ How does this purpose influence individuals and the learning community as a whole?
    - ✓ How do individuals and the learning community influence the intended purpose?
    - ✓ How does this connect to, and influence, our choice of literacy pedagogy?

■ Are the results we seek in alignment with our purpose, philosophy of education, and classroom practice?
  ✓ What do we see that is inherently good and already working for us?
  ✓ What changes can we envision and implement for further alignment?

Literacy leaders are agents of social change. Learning and using systems thinking brings into being healthy individuals and learning communities. We value people within systems collaborating and working in self-directed ways, fully in charge of navigating their own learning. We also value empowerment, and therefore work in ways to ensure no individual is marginalized because of poorly aligned purpose, philosophy, and practice. Our deepest and most important work as literacy leaders is to prioritize the health and wellness of our literacy community as a whole.

Next, we turn our attention toward understanding the role of narrative inquiry and experience as integral to literacy leadership for change.

Narrative Inquiry, Experience, and Literacy Leadership

In Chapter 1, we considered the ways in which policy, research, and practice shape life in classrooms and schools. We described current trends and their influence on the day-to-day work we set out to accomplish as literacy leaders.

The main focus of these trends in education is to maximize student achievement. Another result of shifting policy, research, and practice is that we grow more and more accustomed to quantitative methodology, assessment, and evaluation. Scientifically based reading research, evidence-based teaching, data-driven instruction, and standardized assessment surely develop our capacity for quantitative reasoning! This is wonderful for us as we continue to refine our minds, talents, and skills. Remember, we are always growing. However, as literacy leaders, we need to consciously balance our quantitative thinking with the qualitative. Let us explain.

Literacy leaders are inherently interested in life. We are fascinated—and sometimes stymied—by learning and teaching, as we spend our time in dialogue and collaboration with colleagues and students. What is the *essence*, then, of what we are actually doing? We believe that literacy leaders are in the business of studying life in schools. Through dialogue and collaboration, we are busy collecting stories that reveal how learning, teaching, and leadership are experienced by the people living and working in our local contexts.

This is narrative inquiry and the heart of narrative inquiry is *experience*. We don't mean "experience" defined as the number of years teaching, leading, or learning; nor the mastery of any particular set of skills. Experience in our literacy-leadership context is defined as the moment-by-moment events taking place in our classrooms and schools—the happenings. And it is our interpretation of these happenings that we study. As humans, we turn our lived experiences into stories that we share with others, and this happens all the time through our daily conversations. By paying attention to the stories shared, literacy leaders are able to understand current reality as they experience it, and as experienced by colleagues and students.

Through collaborative work, literacy leaders are able to help colleagues and students use their own stories as templates or texts for learning. Stories help us better understand how learning, leadership, and change are experienced. Vibrant, life-enhancing communities reflect experience through diverse, multiple perspectives. Understanding and appreciating the stories people share shapes new futures, influencing the ways in which people gain momentum to learn, grow, and develop.

We must change our structures, routines, practices, and policies to resonate with the work that needs to happen in collaborative learning communities. Therefore, literacy leaders need to

- value stories as a rich source of qualitative data;
- acquire the ability to frame questions to elicit honest, authentic stories;
- feel comfortable inquiring more deeply into the lives of colleagues and students to better their lives and the life of the organization as a whole;
- work from a source of empathy and compassion when seeking stories and helping others to learn from their stories;
- understand that stories are made up of past, present, and future thinking and that our role is to appreciate *all* the feelings and experiences described;
- recognize how beliefs and values resonate within stories and appreciate the multiple perspectives that are discovered;
- practice active listening to understand someone's experience *and* how words are used to convey the experience;
- teach others how to frame the positive—what is working—and carry the strategies that are positive and working well as possible solutions to difficult situations; and
- be comfortable laying narrative inquiry alongside quantitative thinking for a holistic assessment and evaluation of current reality.

As literacy leaders, we need to know how educators, administrators, and students directly experience the culture of literacy leadership specific to any local context. Valuing the personal, truthful, authentic knowledge of individual and collective experience is a powerful lever for creative change. This information is really a description of current reality. Naming the results we are seeking as literacy leaders is only one step in any change process. It is imperative to know and understand, in truth, what the current reality is to gain momentum for change.

To illustrate the value of narrative inquiry in action, we asked a dear colleague, Linda Sullivan, to reflect upon her life as a literacy leader. In this exploration, we posed a series of questions to better understand Linda's experience. We intentionally look to Linda's beliefs, perceptions, and ways of knowing as connected to literacy leadership and value them as a rich, vibrant, and primary source into which we can glean insight and generate ideas for personal growth and systems-level transformation. Our questions are in bold type. Linda's reflections are italicized.

How are you experiencing the current culture of literacy leadership?

I have experienced literacy leadership as a teacher leader and as a colleague through school-wide and district-wide professional learning communities (PLCs), through participation with literacy coaches and professional staff developers, and through collaboration with colleagues. My experiences in these areas have varied from what I would view as effective (resulting in exploring more effective teaching practices in my classroom) to ineffective (resulting in walking away feeling empty and confused). The cultural attitudes within these venues have also been varied, from openness and willingness toward new and different ideas to resistance. The current culture varies from leadership that focuses on teachers becoming proficient in effective teaching practices to having teachers do nothing more than complete a task.

How do you experience the role of literacy leader? What is it like for you being a model and therefore steward of literacy leadership?

I experience the role with mixed feelings and my role has been inconsistent. At times I enjoy the work. I enjoy being a model, I enjoy talking about my work, and I enjoy getting feedback so I might improve in my own practices as well as being effective in my collaborations with colleagues. When I feel the literacy work and the collaboration are effective (therefore benefiting my students and contributing to a progressive teaching culture), I feel a sense of accomplishment and motivation.

At times I also experience frustration. Although during our literacy work we talk about higher expectations/rigor, sometimes our conversations continue to focus on questions such as "What can we do so they get the right answer?" or "How can we get them to do what we're trying to get them to do?" rather than focusing on student thinking. It is during these times that it is apparent that we do not have common understandings about what good teaching looks like, leaving me to feel not only frustration, but ineffective as a literacy teacher, as I have not been successful in facilitating conversations that focus on core competencies and what it looks like to teach those competencies.

How do you experience changing, growing, and learning within the context of the current system of professional development?

I think the current system of professional development means well. In my experience, we have moved from sending teachers to various workshops without common intent to having district coaches, literacy consultants, and PLCs, both in district and across our tri-district.

In the past couple of years, I think the system of professional development has deteriorated in our district. We began with having coaches on-site and consultants coming in to work with coaches and staff. Demo lessons in classrooms were conducted; workshops allowed teachers to ask questions and discuss their concerns with certain practices or changes; professional discourse was encouraged; and there was talk of doing learning walks and true lesson studies.

The past two years have shown a different professional development path. PLCs were put in place, but not as real PLCs. They are venues for administrative agendas with expected outcomes based on district goals. Within this current system, I have felt forced to change some of my practices in a manner that I do not see benefiting my students. Discussion about these concerns has been discouraged by redirecting conversations back to the agenda. Therefore, there has not been positive change, learning, or growth based on this model of professional development.

How do you experience changing, growing, and learning in the context of your moment-to-moment literacy-leadership work?

The change, growth, and learning that occur are due to my initiative to seek information and conversation outside the parameters of the district-provided professional development. I talk with other professionals interested in the work of teaching; I read professional-development literature; and I collaborate with colleagues who have the same understandings so that our conversations can move us forward in improving our literacy practices. I "try" these approaches/methods in my classroom and sometimes I share my experiences with my colleagues and sometimes I work alone in evaluating the new approaches. The collegial "tribe" I am speaking of is small, so I experience changing, growing, and learning in a somewhat lonely manner.

How do you experience communication within the broad culture of literacy leadership?

Communication within the broad culture of literacy leadership (defining "broad culture" as "school wide, district wide, and within the tri-district") is limited in the sense of progressive thinking.

How do you experience communication within the context of your own literacy-leadership work?

Communication within my own literacy work is more effective (in my opinion) than in the broader culture. I believe this is because, in my own literacy work, I collaborate with those who approach me interested in discussing their work—and I seek out those with whom I have commonalities—resulting in our conversations (and ultimate collaboration of work) having effective and, in some cases, powerful outcomes.

How do you experience movement through the reflection process as a literacy leader?

The reflective process has not been a piece of our literacy work in our current professional development structure. On a personal level, it is limited. I think I reflect on my own work, as a leader and a classroom teacher, but I am not sure what questions I should be asking myself, and our PLCs are not conducive to this type of group reflection.

How do you experience working through difficult situations as a literacy leader?

This has not been a positive area. Recently I have not been involved as a leader in the broader sense. I have been expected to be a leader in my grade unit and in tri-district meetings. The difficult situations have been in what I might call "shut-down" in discussing progressive thinking. So, I believed it was necessary to take a step back and angle conversations to where people were in their literacy thinking, and then pose some questions that might get the conversations moving forward. Patience with the conversations and gently probing the ideas are what seemed to be the most effective. However, I experienced walking away from these situations with a feeling that the status quo remained in place. Change is really slow.

How did you experience this questioning process? What was this experience like for you?

This questioning process was difficult because my literacy-leadership experience has diminished over the past two years. The questioning also revealed that my literacy frustration has grown due to that diminished role. Thinking back over the literacy work I have done makes me want to approach literacy collaborations in a way that has us engaging in a continual process of studying our teaching views and values, our methods of teaching, and studying our students and their work in order to strengthen our roles as educators. As I worked through these questions and reflected on my school district and the work that has been done, the fact that literacy work is everyone's responsibility (across all content areas) has been reaffirmed, along with my belief that all students (every learner) must have access to the thinking work that strengthens literacy skills. This, therefore, makes me think about our "special-ed" services in our schools and the ever-growing importance of including those teachers in our literacy work. Along with reflecting on the progress and road blocks of literacy leadership, this questioning process has raised some additional concerns about the importance of moving forward with this work.

We would like to first thank Linda for her willingness to share her experiences and reflective thinking with honesty and grace. This is the hallmark of respectful, trusting, and collaborative relationships. What does Linda's experience and reflective thinking open us up to realize? In valuing Linda's experience, we come to understand that she

- is an experienced literacy leader;
- easily differentiates effective and noneffective professional learning experiences;
- readily perceives fluctuations in school culture and fluctuations regarding the purpose of professional learning;
- has felt accomplished and motivated within the context of particular learning and leadership conditions;
- is able to quickly pinpoint where common literacy knowledge and understanding do converge, and also to identify gaps where convergence breaks down;
- may be feeling frustrated because she is not being challenged to delve deeply enough into her own learning to work differently with her students;
- sees her environment as rich in resources;
- views her learning and work as co-opted by administrative agendas that do not align with effective learning, growth, and development;
- is self-directed and initiates networking to learn beyond the environment in which she physically works;
- experiences professional learning as lonely;
- finds broad communication lacking in progressive thought (Linda does communicate with those who share common interests in education);
- has not engaged in professional learning that is reflective in nature;
- is open to learning how to develop questions to guide reflective thinking;
- perceives PLCs as not conducive to reflective thinking;
- understands how to flex her questioning strategies and conversation starters to meet the learning edge of colleagues;
- is keenly aware of how the status quo is perpetuated in spite of professional learning situations;
- values holding a larger role in literacy leadership;
- advocates for studying teaching views, values, and methods; advocates for studying students and their work; understands the process is mutually enhancing for development and growth of both student and teacher;
- believes in shared literacy leadership;
- values inclusion of special education teachers in the professional learning process; and
- advocates for moving forward with literacy-leadership work.

In studying Linda's account of her experiences and reflective thinking, we come away with a rich tapestry of valuable information. There are serious implications for change at work here! Because we know, understand, value, and empathize with Linda, we are in the position to cocreate change. Knowing how she experiences literacy leadership, we can engender—*do more of*—what is working for her and alter aspects that could be working better. Above all else, by connecting to Linda's experience, we can see that a responsive and respectful environment for learning and leading must be established. Creating clarity in common language, purpose, and vision is the container for all next steps. Learning needs to be the work of—the shared responsibility of—administrators, teachers, and students. There are many, many points of positive departure here for change. Honesty and respect cultivate the depth learning communities require. How might you collaborate with Linda to cocreate a learning community that will engage her on a deeper level so she once again is motivated and challenged toward a new learning edge?

Narrative inquiry is such an integral process to literacy leadership. Because learning, teaching, and leadership are inherently tied to who we are as people, how we think and behave, we need a process for changing our work to that which is humanistic and real—one that allows us to dig deep. Narrative inquiry as a way of thinking and being is really a bridge for literacy leaders. It helps us see that stories are the playing field of change. We need to be on the field to help transform the field.

When literacy leaders understand what narrative inquiry is, and how to use it, we will be well on our way to creating renaissance communities. We *can* bring these life-enhancing communities into being. We hope you hold an enhanced understanding of the purpose and value of collecting and studying life stories.

Across this chapter so far, we explored systems thinking; considered the necessity of aligning purpose, philosophy, and pedagogy; and opened ourselves to narrative inquiry. To complete our paradigm of change, we are turning our attention now to appreciative coaching.

Appreciative Coaching and Literacy Leadership

As literacy leaders, we have experienced "literacy-leadership blocks" at one time or another in our professional lives, affecting us in the same way painters or writers are suddenly cut off from their own ability or inspiration in their craft. Passion and purpose abound, yet we find ourselves feeling like we need a larger container for our work and that our skills are not sufficient for the new work that needs to be accomplished in complex learning environments. At first, the feelings that confront us are truly disturbing—and so is the self-talk that accompanies them. It goes something like this:

> I'm inadequate, totally confused, and unskilled! I'm too small for the task that needs to be accomplished. I can't do this. Maybe it's just a slump. Oh, okay, it's

just me working from a deficit model and I can see the glass—nope, not half full, it's not even a quarter of the way full! Wait, there's not even a drop in the glass! Nothing that I do is working.

Pretty bleak, huh?

Well, we can look at this self-talk, this story, and stay in the negative. Or, we can look at it and find the humor and humanity in the situation. We opt for humor and humanity. In fact, we make the conscious choice to focus on how the experience brings forth positives for us and the meaning it provides for our next steps. We are not looking at this story through rose-colored glasses and brushing off the hurt that comes along with the feelings of relinquishing who we used to be as we fight the need to try something new. We are honoring the reality of the hurt and using it to build momentum for positive change. So, in looking at our shared story, what are the positives? In the self-talk just described, we are reflective people. We have the sense that something more is needed. We understand that the task of change is huge and complex. We see and recognize that deficit-model thinking creeps into our work even when we try to keep it at bay. We admit when we are seeing the glass as really empty. And above all, we are empowered to express our truth through authenticity and honesty. *We are open and willing and needing support.* But what kind of support do we need?

We may not be looking for, or believe that we need, a leader to teach us more about literacy strategies. In fact, we do this very well on our own as self-directed learners. But, maybe the kind of learning we do need—the kind of support we need—is to learn how to tap into our strengths to achieve the more difficult-to-acquire results we really, really want and desire. So, what is the actual strategy that a literacy leader would use in this situation? We need to explain that it isn't a strategy at all—at least not in the traditional sense. Instead, we need to approach this next concept as a way of thinking and being that gently puts to use systems thinking, narrative inquiry, and appreciative leadership. The literacy leader needs to be an appreciative coach!

Appreciative inquiry, appreciative leadership, and appreciative coaching are prominent ideas within the field of organizational development and change. The efficacy of this work is long standing, research based, and often used to create positive change in business, government, psychology and the social services, and education. Literacy leaders will truly benefit from studying its philosophy and practical applications to create a larger—and more humane—container for our work in classrooms and schools. We need to synthesize the key ideas as a coaching framework and apply it to literacy leadership as a way of thinking, being, and creating within the context of our work. The key ideas of appreciative inquiry, leadership, and coaching are to be shared, used, and celebrated throughout the organization—it is not the property solely of literacy leaders as the secret to literacy-leadership work. It is important to understand that, as with systems thinking and narrative inquiry, appreciative coaching is an applied philosophy and process used as we mentor and coach each other in partnership and collaboration.

Within the context of literacy leadership for change, everyone is a literacy leader. Therefore, everyone—colleagues and students alike—needs to learn the knowledge and skills to be appreciative coaches. Literacy leaders know how to access and encourage others to learn literacy-related content. What we need to revolutionize is the way we go about the work of helping others, using systems thinking, narrative inquiry, and appreciative coaching. While we cannot provide an in-depth understanding of appreciative inquiry, leadership, and coaching here because the knowledge base is deep and wide (and needs to be read as such), what we can do here is provide a list of recommendations for literacy leaders regarding how to begin thinking about appreciative coaching as a necessary component of literacy leadership for change.

To begin, we should start with shared definitions. Appreciative inquiry "is a high-engagement strengths-based process through which people collaboratively reinvent the vision, mission, strategy, culture, and identity of their organization or community" (Whitney, Trosten-Bloom, & Rader, 2010, p. xvi). Therefore, appreciative leadership "is the relational capacity to mobilize creative potential and turn it into positive power—to set in motion positive ripples of confidence, energy, enthusiasm, and performance—to make a positive difference in the world" (p. 3). It is easy to see that this body of work resonates so well with how we are trying to approach our work each day as literacy leaders. Appreciative inquiry and leadership offer a philosophical and practical framework to guide the way we conduct literacy-leadership work each day. What we draw from this framework is a way of coaching others for peak performance and positive, creative change.

In essence, as literacy leaders, we need to frame "coaching" not as a full-blown job description, but as the way we approach our conversations and collaboration. We need to believe that every conversation and action taken alters reality in ways that may be good or bad. No matter what, conversation and events are taking place in classrooms and schools. How we approach these conversations and events needs to be part of what we study in literacy leadership—as we do with stories. We recommend that literacy leaders infuse five core strategies into their work as agents of change. Literacy leaders are engaged in "coaching work" when they

1. inquire into the lives of colleagues and students to learn their strengths, talents, desires, and success stories and they find out what people *really* want;

2. ask colleagues and students to share stories that illuminate strengths, effective practices, and achievement;

3. include many people—many voices—in dialogue and collaboration while enhancing the quality of how people relate to each other;

4. inspire people to work from what is already positive, to achieve beyond the status quo in ways that are realistic for colleagues and students while living and relating appreciatively; and

5. model integrity.

These five core strategies of appreciative inquiry and leadership provide us with a new way of thinking about the coaching skills we need as literacy leaders to cultivate life-enhancing learning communities. Literacy leaders also benefit by drawing upon the work of Orem, Binkert, and Clancy (2007), as these experts in the field of appreciative inquiry provide an in-depth understanding of appreciative coaching processes. Four key processes are listed here for you as applied literacy-leadership work. When literacy leaders coach colleagues and students moment by moment, our practice includes helping others to

- discover and appreciate the good that *already* exists in their experiences, talents, skills, and ability;

- dream—expand their thinking—about what it is they *really* want to create in their classroom and school environment;

- design a picture or vision of the results they want to create and action steps needed; and

- achieve their destiny by celebrating current work that is realizing the dream.

This is the deeper and most authentic work of literacy leadership!

We now turn our attention to an example of an appreciative interview—appreciative coaching—in action. Dana Jackson, our colleague and dear friend, shares her thinking and experience of literacy leadership with us as she engages in a conversation with Kristine. Kristine comes to this conversation with appreciative inquiry and leadership as her knowledge base and uses this knowledge to frame questions that encourage honest and respectful dialogue. Kristine is not interested in changing Dana. Kristine is interested in discovering what Dana values. This insight is what influences how *Kristine* changes, flexing the way she needs to support Dana as opposed to how she would offer support for someone else. Within this context, the essence of literacy leadership shifts to differentiating the way we design support systems for colleagues and students! This is honest literacy-leadership work.

Please know that Dana and Kristine's conversation is ongoing, in person, and online! It is never finished. At times it is formal; other times it is informal. The dialogue is always growing and changing. We are able to share with you an aspect of this interview that models a more formal stance. Kristine's contribution is in bold type. Dana's contribution is italicized.

Dana, what gives life to you now, in this moment, as a literacy leader?

Looking at how schools will implement the new Common Core State Standards is interesting to me right now. I think one of the most interesting topics within the Core is text complexity and vocabulary acquisition. Teachers tend to be married to books, but I think there will, hopefully, be some real discussions about whether the texts teachers are married to are appropriate for those grade levels. Just because a book is long, or you have great lesson plans for the book, doesn't mean that the book may be complex enough for the given grade. I also say vocabulary acquisition, because I don't think schools have yet to pin down a meaningful way to get at vocabulary at the secondary level. Rote memorization doth not a large vocabulary make.

Can you tell me more about your vision for these kinds of discussions that you'd like to have with others?

It's not that I would like to have these discussions per se; it's that there needs to be more authentic discussion in education if you truly want to improve student learning. So much of what I see tends to be haphazard; there's an assumption that if you put teachers together, they will suddenly start to talk about improving student learning. That isn't so at all. There needs to be deliberate, thought-filled action if the intention is to improve teachers with the purpose of improving student learning.

Describe a high point or peak experience in your life as a literacy leader.

Perhaps becoming the literacy coach at the high school level. I say this because I don't know if it allowed me to lead where literacy was concerned. Yes, I supported teachers, but oftentimes it had very little to do with improving student literacy.

What is your picture or vision of effective literacy leadership?

I don't know yet. I don't know if a model of coaching, at least at the secondary level, is effective. I'm still attempting to determine where the literacy leadership needs to begin.

What do you value most about yourself, your relationships, and the nature of your work?

I value my desire to think deeply about things. I also love to learn and I hope to transfer that enthusiasm to students. I don't know if it always works, but that has been my goal to some degree. I think it's important that people think purposefully, particularly in this complex world today.

What one or two things do you want more of in your life as a literacy leader?

More time and more opportunities to work with all the players involved in improving the literacy of our adolescents. I think we as a community who are involved in the education of our youth, including the youth themselves, don't interact in a real way. Much of what we do is affectation (PDs, parent conferences, common planning, evaluations, meetings). A lot of it is talk because there is some sort of political agenda (both real and imaginary) that must be executed. The only ones who suffer in the long run are the students. Enough of the idle chatter and let's get to the work of learning.

We'd like to thank Dana for her contribution. Her dialogue is honest, open, and real. As a whole, this "slice of life" shows what Dana is thinking and opens up so many possibilities for how we as literacy leaders can change. Kristine comes to the conversation with only one agenda—to support Dana in the achievement of her own goals. In supporting Dana, Kristine needs to frame questions that are deep and expansive. She frames the conversation to open up *possibility*. Kristine is also aware of the need to flex inner responsiveness and an outer responsiveness. Not only is she responsible for her own inner change, Kristine needs to also take action to change structures of the learning environment to enhance learning, growth, and development.

Appreciative coaching is much like narrative inquiry. As literacy leaders, we draw from what is honest, real, and working. We pull forward what is already life-enhancing to further shape our inner and outer environments. Appreciative coaching is literacy leadership. Folding this into our approach empowers everyone involved. We will be working from a core self that is most authentic, least marginalizing, antioppressive, and true to our prime objective—respectful transformation.

Closing Thoughts

Collaborative learning communities are complex, living systems. Authentic and respectful change will come into being as literacy leaders engage colleagues and students in systems thinking, aligning purpose, philosophy, and pedagogy, sharing stories of lived experience, and engaging in our deepest work through appreciative coaching. This is the change paradigm for literacy leadership! Although the work is vast, we, like Van Gogh, value the deeper terrain of change and know that our best work comes into being through the synchronicity of small, patient steps.

At this time, we invite you to hear the voices of literacy leaders in the field as you read and contemplate The Ethical Literacy Leader and Critical Voices features in this chapter. Following each feature are questions in the Cultivate Your Leadership Skills section to prompt your thinking as you work toward portraying a paradigm for change in your context. To read more about all of our contributors' backgrounds, see the About the Contributors section of this text.

The Ethical Literacy Leader
The "A for Effort" Dilemma
—JILL LEWIS-SPECTOR

Jill is vice-president of the International Reading Association and has served on its board of directors (2004–2007), as president of IRA's LEADER Special Interest Group, and as chair of the IRA Governmental Relations Committee.

Developing literacy skills of underprepared college freshmen has been a personal and professional challenge during my nearly 40 years of teaching. The ethical dilemmas I have confronted were initially mine alone, especially when failing a student might mean the end of that student's college career; passing indicated that I believed the student would be successful in college. More troubling was that even if students demonstrated comprehension of the department-selected texts used in our remedial reading courses, I knew these materials bore little resemblance to the complex texts students would be expected to comprehend in later academic studies. I was a good teacher; the students had good intentions and many worked hard in our classes. But I felt some would have found community or technical college vocational programs more beneficial.

The challenges my dilemmas posed became even more apparent when I became department chair. In an effort to meet budget needs, the university began admitting large numbers of remedial students, and the number of our department's remedial reading courses grew significantly. As chair, however, I had the potential to lead reform efforts with colleagues that addressed what I considered an unethical university admissions practice: encouraging so many underprepared students to pass through what I saw as a "revolving door," taking some students' tuition for one or two semesters while knowing, from the start, they would not succeed. As department leader, and to make any reform inroads, I needed to discuss the

issue with colleagues both in and outside the department, gather data with them to confirm concerns, and work with multiple stakeholders to gain support for reform, brainstorm ideas, and implement those we agreed upon.

The first step was to discuss my concerns with my department, explaining the ethical conflict I felt. I hold honesty as a core value, and I believed it was dishonest to pass students who showed little promise of academic success, in spite of enrollment consequences for the department and the university. There were nine members of the department and, as we talked, most expressed a similar personal conflict. We decided to first investigate how students fared both in and subsequent to our basic literacy courses, and then to use the results of this action research to motivate other stakeholders and initiate university-wide discussion. Department members assisted with this research. We found that nearly one-third of our students did not successfully complete the basic-skills literacy courses and were consequently discharged from our university. Furthermore, of the remaining two-thirds, only one-third actually completed a college degree within six years at our university; the remaining one-third were no longer enrolled.

These findings enabled me, as chair, to move ahead and connect with other stakeholders who also might be affected by reform, especially those in the English department, who typically taught basic writing skills to the same students in our Reading for College classes. One writing-skills instructor in the English department,

Walter Glospie, and I had frequently conferred about mutual students. I approached him first. He concurred with my department's concerns and was not surprised by our research findings. Walter became the message bearer to his department that soon agreed that our departments would work together on developing a vision for reform, one that was flexible enough for revisiting and revising when necessary. I was encouraged that out-of-department stakeholders were now on board!

After much discussion with our respective departments' colleagues on an action plan, Walter and I spearheaded designing a unique course, Reading and Writing across the Disciplines (RWAD). Three-person RWAD faculty teams would be made of one member each from the Literacy Education department, English department, and another content field (general studies) department (e.g., sociology, economics, media). The content faculty member would provide the lead for the team by selecting the content course textbook; the writing and reading instructors would use this text as a basis for instruction. We would meet throughout the semester to revisit course design, and to confer with our respective departments as we continued to reform the skills classes.

This course design meant we needed to bring members of other departments into the conversation and obtain their willingness to participate. As Walter and I spoke with general studies faculty, what became evident was that the content professors did not realize that many of their freshmen students could not comprehend their texts; they had been attributing students' low grades to a lack of effort. The faculty became intrigued by the idea of a team approach, and professors from the sciences and social sciences departments signed on. The administration granted a small incentive to faculty—0.5 credit for teamwork.

As minimal as it was, this release time for planning signaled administrative support for our reforms.

It has been nearly 20 years since Reading and Writing across the Disciplines was first offered, and it does not look exactly as it did when Walter and I designed it. But, the team approach is still in effect, and outcomes for students are better. They encounter academic text in their remedial courses, and they know that a team of professors is working together to address students' literacy needs. I cannot say that my dilemma is completely resolved, but the reality-based instruction makes it easier to identify which underprepared students will succeed in college and to grade more honestly. I see more students graduating who had been in our RWAD classes as compared to the number who remained in college following a semester in our previous remedial reading courses. I feel that, as the department chair at the time, I had provided the leadership needed to address an ethical concern and to provide leadership to faculty of several departments that produced an outcome that better serves our students.

Cultivate Your Leadership Skills

1. In what ways can a systems-thinking lens be applied within the context of this college experience? How does this systems-thinking lens help stakeholders meet the needs of learners?
2. Considering the author's point of view, which purpose of schooling and philosophy of education is evidenced? What is the link between purpose, philosophy, project implementation, and learning outcomes?
3. How is sustainability—sustainable leadership and sustainable learning—positioned as an ethical imperative within the context of this experience?

Critical Voices

Our Collaborative Journey of Change

—SANDRA ATHANS

Sandra is National Board–certified in Literacy: Reading—Language Arts. She is a fourth-grade classroom teacher in the Chittenango Central school district in central New York.

Our literacy instruction needed a severe change! Results from our fourth-grade state language arts assessment emphasized the everyday struggles we witnessed in our classrooms. Nearly half of all students within our six fourth-grade classes squeaked by or did not meet state proficiency standards. Beyond this, we instinctively knew that many of our students could not decipher a grade-level reading passage on their own; victims of decoding debacles, fluency floundering, or comprehension conundrums, they were not privy to any of the joys of reading. This had to change.

As classroom teachers, we shared an obligation to *significantly* improve our students' reading comprehension. This united us at the onset of our journey and overshadowed the differences among us: experience, age, knowledge, and beliefs and attitudes about reading instruction. Yet, cementing us together for the duration of our journey was our deep sense of ownership; for the most part, finding a solution was *our* responsibility. We were the ones in the classroom trenches—though we welcomed the support of our specialists and administrators.

Gathering Knowledge to Direct Our Professional Development

Without a clear sense of direction, our first step was to gather information on best practices. Some of us attended local and regional conferences. As funds were slim, we wrote grants and pooled resources whenever possible.

Others reached out to colleagues in neighboring districts to arrange site visits. We read articles and books, and we met as a team every Thursday morning for half an hour before school in order to debrief and devise our next moves.

After careful reflection, we selected guided reading as our focus. It was an approach with proven success at lower elementary grades. We also wished to integrate science and social studies themes into our reading instruction. We hoped this immersion might help shore up weaknesses in our students' content-area reading skills.

Throughout this part of our journey, we shared information regularly, passing noteworthy materials among the six of us. "Use This as You Wish" became the catchphrase we scrawled across a sticky note router. The words captured the spirit of our teacher-initiated, teacher-led collaboration. The message stressed flexibility, encouraged creativity, and was sincere.

Action Research

Integrating our plan came next. We retained elements of our whole-class instruction and introduced small-group differentiated instruction, which was critical for scaffolding our readers. We also allotted time for students' independent practice. We then watched to see what would happen.

Our problems sprang up like weeds: we were short of materials; new classroom management issues demanded our attention;

and our commitment to achieve equity for *all* readers seemed a relentless juggling act. Still, our team stuck together and shared resources, helpful ideas, and backbone support with the same collaborative spirit.

As a result, eventually our challenges were replaced by glimmers of progress. We were encouraged and hoped to verify our students' gains through action research. We conducted our first study using a competitive grant we were awarded by our regional teaching center. Happily, our findings supported our students' improvements.

Taking the Lead

As we progressed, we shaped and refined our practices and created instructional resources using our collaborative approach. Read-Along Guides, a student comprehension tool, helped us identify how best to target, differentiate, and scaffold our instruction to meet the needs of each student. Literacy Bins, our unique take on literacy centers, fostered students' self-directed learning and complemented our instructional approaches. We studied these tools in our classrooms and refined them as needed.

Where We Are Today

Since the start of our journey, 10 years have passed. In that time, we were awarded 15 grants for professional development, classroom research, and/or the development of instructional materials. We also established cross-grade-level teams in our district and expanded a collaborative network of teachers outside of our district.

Our students continue to improve, as our test results and our classroom observations confirm. We continue to meet every Thursday morning, despite changes in our team membership. And we still share ideas and materials as well as challenges and new journeys. Our catchphrase "Use This as You Wish" still appears on our sticky note routers, yet it has gone digital and is more often the subject of our electronic correspondence.

We are *highly* indebted to our struggling students. Clearly, the need to change our literacy practices 10 years ago provided the impetus for us to master today's troubleshooting processes. Our teacher-initiated, teacher-led model of collaboration continues to hold up under pressure and is currently in use as we address the Common Core Standards. Change can be very, very good, especially when tackled collaboratively.

Cultivate Your Leadership Skills

1. In what ways does this vignette demonstrate collaborative literacy leadership? How did this collaborative approach influence the school as a living system?
2. How is literacy leadership positioned as experiential learning within this system?
3. What patterns of influence can you see as the purpose of education, philosophy, and literacy practices intersect in this vignette?
4. How is literacy leadership sustainable within this context? What is working well? How else might you influence the system?

Questions for Reflection and Discussion

1. Reflect upon the current reality of literacy leadership in your school. How is systems thinking already in place? How else might it evolve?

2. As a literacy leader, how does your thinking and behavior influence the school environment? How are you influenced by the school environment? What changes would you like to make to increase health and wellness for self, others, and the school?

3. How will you further your own understanding and mastery of systems thinking, narrative inquiry, and appreciative coaching?

Practical Applications

How might this chapter apply to your teaching context and experience? Try these activities:

Classroom Activity

Choose one week of the school year and devote it to thinking about systems. Through reflective journaling, consider how your thinking and behavior influence your students. What do you notice? In turn, how are students influencing you and each other in the classroom? How is everyone influenced by—*and influencing*—curriculum, instruction, and assessment? What do you notice? What changes would you like to make? How might you teach your students systems thinking to shift the classroom environment in positive ways?

Professional Development Activity

Appreciative inquiry is such an interesting field of study! Organize a book club to better understand the philosophy and practical application of appreciative inquiry, appreciative leadership, and appreciative coaching. As you read, keep a list of key points to share with your book club colleagues. When you meet, share the key points you find so valuable and applicable to creating change in your local context. Discuss ways you can implement appreciative inquiry and coaching so that it becomes integral to literacy leadership.

References

Allen, J. (2006) *Becoming a literacy leader: Supporting learning and change.* Portland, ME: Stenhouse Publishers.

Orem, S. L., Binkert, J., & Clancy, A. L. (2007). *Appreciative coaching: A positive process for change.* San Francisco, CA: Jossey-Bass.

VanDerHeyden, A. M., Witt, J. C., & Gilbertson, D. A. (2007). Multi-year evaluation of the effects of a response to intervention (RTI) model on identification of children for special education. *Journal of School Psychology, 45,* 225–256.

VanDerHeyden, A. M., Witt, J. C., & Naquin, G. (2003). The development and validation of a process for screening and referrals to special education. *School Psychology Review, 32,* 204–227.

Whitney, D., Trosten-Bloom, A., & Rader, K. (2010). *Appreciative leadership: Focus on what works to drive winning performance and build a thriving organization.* New York: McGraw-Hill.

Zinn, L. M. (2004). Exploring your philosophical orientation. In M. W. Galbraith (Ed.), *Adult learning methods: A guide for effective instruction* (pp. 39–74). Malabar, FL: Krieger Publishing Company.

Painting a Vision of Literacy Leadership

"I dream of painting and then I paint my dream."

—VINCENT VAN GOGH

If you were Van Gogh, what would your "dream of painting" a vision of literacy leadership include? How would you paint your dream? Now that we have re-framed the culture of literacy leadership and defined the professional standards that support literacy leadership in today's schools in Chapter 1, we will consider what a portrait of literacy leadership looks like in a school.

We'll begin by visualizing a portrait of goals for literacy leaders. Once goals are established, how do we achieve them through professional development? And what roles do professional communities of practice play in literacy leadership? Finally, we'll see how The Ethical Literacy Leader and Critical Voices features apply the topics in this chapter to authentic contexts and experiences.

A Portrait of Goals for Literacy Leaders

Most of us can remember belonging to a group—an athletic team, perhaps—that exceeded beyond its members' own expectations because their energy was tapped by the high expectations of a coach or leader. Maybe, too, you remember a certain teacher who expected you to do the best you could do, driving you to do more than you thought you could. Rather than tie you down like Gulliver during his travels, that teacher promoted excellence. With this vision in mind, let's consider how we as literacy leaders might cut the ties that bind our "Gullivers" by contemplating our expectations for ourselves and those we guide. Read this chapter's Response to Intervention (RTI) and the Literacy Leader feature by Dawn Hamlin for suggestions on this topic.

Response to Intervention (RTI) and the Literacy Leader

Explicit and Intense: Welcome to the Emergency Room

—DAWN HAMLIN

Dawn is currently an assistant professor at SUNY College at Oneonta. She is a former special education teacher who taught in both traditional public schools and residential facilities.

Response to intervention (RTI) is meant to provide increasingly individualized and intensive interventions as one moves up the tier levels. In this regard, it is a lot like an emergency room for struggling students who are not on target for certain skills.

In this emergency room scenario, the literacy leaders and other RTI team members play roles similar to intake coordinators. If students do not pass the "well check" visit (i.e., the initial screening), the literacy leaders and other team members must triage the students to hone in on effective and efficient interventions.

While there may be many different interventions that have research support for being effective, literacy leaders must choose the most efficient and highly documented evidence-based practices. Time is a critical constraint. Like the emergency room, students should not be placed on a particular tier for an undetermined amount of time. Rather, placement should be temporary. Students should be rapidly cared for and then sent back to the typical classroom setting. If the response to initial treatment is ineffective, then they should be moved up into more critical care levels.

As students move up through different tier levels, they should receive increasingly intense, strategic, explicit, evidence-based interventions that target a few critical areas. The goal then would be for the students to hopefully return to lower tier levels and/or regular classroom instruction. One critical caveat for all instructional tiers is that RTI will not be effective if literacy leaders or other team members fail to implement interventions with high levels of procedural fidelity (McLesky & Waldron, 2011).

Remember from Chapter 1 that we reframed literacy leadership as

embodied as community cultural development, offering a rich canvas of ideology, mission, and vision. It is a framework of possibility and carries an ethos of liberation, transformation, and human and cultural development. It is a cultural container for educational philosophy, inspiration, artistry, and responsive pedagogy that is colorful, vibrant, dynamic, and diverse. (p. 7–8)

Literacy leaders are the students, families, teacher assistants, teachers, specialists, school staff, administrators, board of education members, and community members who socially construct literacy education. Using this broad perception to identify the literacy leaders in a district, what do we see as their universal or common goals? Based on our experiences and a review of the professional standards that support literacy leaders in Chapter 1, we propose literacy leaders seek to work with teachers to

- improve their knowledge, skills, and dispositions;
- facilitate the improvement of all students' performances; and
- develop the type of school culture that reflects the vision of its in-school and beyond-school members: families, local community, and professional communities.

Let's look more closely at each of these three goals.

Goal #1: Literacy Leaders Seek to Improve Evidence-Based Literacy Pedagogy

This goal really consists of improving teaching and basing literacy pedagogy on evidence-based research. Support comes in many forms when the goal is to improve teaching. Effective teaching involves

- having and growing the knowledge one needs about teaching and the content;
- demonstrating the skills one needs to communicate with colleagues and students and to design and implement effective lessons; and
- developing the dispositions to deal with and, if need be, resolve the daily feelings, concerns, and questions of the day.

Sometimes support may take the shape of sharing specific resources or helping teachers make connections between curriculum materials and learning standards. It may involve offering appropriate and timely tips on effective ways to group students so they work to the best of their ability and development. Literacy leaders may be responsible for organizing and arranging for professional development of teachers and may help facilitate meetings of professional learning communities. Teachers may request assistance setting up a research study to investigate an inquiry they have about instruction and learning within the context of their classroom. Literacy leaders seek to meet the learning needs of teachers and staff so literacy pedagogy reflects up-to-date, evidence-based strategies, methods, and approaches that reflect the findings of current research in the field.

Goal #2: Literacy Leaders Seek to Improve the Performance of All Students

The key word here is *all*. Undoubtedly, *all* students need to be given opportunities to succeed. Recently, our school invited Rye Barcott to our campus to speak. Barcott is the author of *It Happened on the Way to War: A Marine's Path to Peace* (2011), a book about his work with families in a slum area of Nairobi, Kenya. After his presentation, I asked him what he saw poverty doing to children. His response was that poverty can strip children of opportunities, leaving them disempowered and unable to break through the boundaries that constrict them. Despite the call to leave no child behind and to provide a quality education to all children, those children who have traditionally been underserved—those from low-income families and underrepresented minorities—continue to perform at the lowest academic levels. They consistently drop out of school more frequently, and they go on to college at lower percentages than their white, middle-class peers (George & Aronson, n.d.). Barcott (2011) would most likely say they have been stripped of opportunities and disempowered.

Furthermore, racial and ethnic segregation continues in the form of inner-city minority schools. Children in schools that consist primarily of minorities often experience less rigorous curricula, are given fewer opportunities for enrichment, are taught by less qualified teachers, and receive funding for fewer resources than their white, middle-class counterparts. Also, research tells us educators have preconceived notions about students based on their belief systems about the roles race, ethnicity, and socioeconomic status play in student performance and achievement (see Johnson, 1992; Kuzborska, 2011; Meltzer & Hamann, 2005; and Woolfolk, Davis, & Pape, 2006). Educators' preconceptions affect their expectations of students' ability to learn. Lowered expectations influence the opportunities educators present for students to succeed.

Whether it is poverty, race, religion, ability, or disability that affects students' performance, we must find ways to advocate for our children so they all are given the same opportunities and are empowered. Literacy leaders need to ignite the minds of all students by cultivating the genius that lies within each teacher and child and challenging the boundaries that tie down our "Gullivers."

Goal #3: Literacy Leaders Seek to Affect School Culture

Cindy's first building principal, Mr. DeVitto, was an ex-professional baseball player. You'd see him out there on the sidelines after school talking with families and the players, wearing the team's baseball cap, cheering on the teams. His passion about baseball, however, was incidental compared to the ardor he demonstrated for the school, its staff and teachers, and the community. It was evident in everything he did and every word he spoke. As a result, he had become a person who was trusted and looked up to. The town and his teachers had faith in him.

A strong literacy leader works like an anthropologist, getting to know "the natives" first, to access the culture of a population before even attempting to suggest any changes (Davis, 2006). Once time has been spent observing, interacting, asking questions, gathering information, and gaining the community's trust—as Mr. DeVitto had—the literacy leaders of a district can begin to understand the history, mores, attitudes, and values of the school and community—encompassing the school board, families, teachers, and students.

Educators often lament about the difficulties of implementing change in a school. However, it can be easier to affect school culture when everyone is on board, is invested, and buys into an idea. Literacy leaders seek to be agents of change to affect school culture in positive ways that reflect the spirit of its members (DuFour, DuFour, & Eaker, 2008). It is important that they persevere and practice patience when the context is more difficult to change. (See how Katie Stover worked with teachers who were initially resistant to her coaching in this chapter's Critical Voices feature.)

A Portrait of Effective Professional Development

How do we as literacy leaders work with others to achieve the literacy goals described in the previous section? One very crucial way is by planning and arranging effective professional development experiences with faculty and staff in a democratic, experiential manner. The National Staff Development Council (n.d.) defines professional development as "a comprehensive, sustained, and intensive approach to improving teachers' and principals' effectiveness in raising student achievement" (http://www.learningforward.org/standfor/definition.cfm). The Elementary and Secondary Education Act (ESEA), in its reauthorization of the No Child Left Behind Act of 2001, states that professional development must be rigorous and include activities that will develop highly qualified teachers. (For the ESEA, go to http://www2.ed.gov/policy/elsec/leg/esea02/pg107.html.) These activities are characterized as those that

- increase teachers' knowledge and skills;
- have a lasting impact on instruction and standards such as the Common Core State Standards (see this chapter's The Common Core State Standards Connection feature);
- are developed collaboratively by teachers, administrators, and families;
- support teachers of students with diverse needs;
- support the learning and uses of technology;
- are evaluated regularly;
- foster teacher research; and
- support communication and interactions with students' families.

Furthermore, these activities may involve forming school-university partnerships to train teachers, and supporting paraprofessionals who want to become certified teachers.

Case Scenarios

Two case scenarios follow. The two schools, Schoharie Elementary and Cobleskill Elementary, are having their annual professional development (PD) day. Students have the day off from school. The day has been reserved to improve teachers' effectiveness and raise student achievement. As you read, think about how these days align with the characteristics identified by ESEA and, as a caring and interested professional, which school's day you would rather attend.

The Common Core State Standards Connection
Continue to Press Toward the Mark
—TRACEY JOHNSON

Tracey's career in education spans over 22 years. She has taught at all educational levels, developed curriculum, provided professional development to persistently low-achieving schools, and mentored teachers. Currently, Tracy is employed at the New York State Education Department.

The Common Core State Standards initiative has made its mark in the educational history of America. The overarching goal or "mark" is to ensure that no matter where students live, they are prepared for success in postsecondary education and the workforce. This huge undertaking has spurred a need to collaborate across states, legislative agencies, and educational institutions to develop instructional materials and resources, provide professional development, and create assessments to ensure the standards are implemented successfully.

It is imperative that educators and local and state policymakers work in tandem to align their goals on key areas that require attention and work as states transition to the standards. Although school districts are faced with dire fiscal constraints, and sometimes opposing societal issues, highly effective instructional programs and learning opportunities must not be compromised. Education agencies and institutions will have to keep their focus and press toward the mark, which is to provide students of the 21st century an education to ensure that they will be successful citizens, and who are college and career ready.

Case Scenario A

PD Day at Schoharie Elementary

It's another professional development day at Schoharie Elementary. The teachers file into the auditorium eager to hear what the latest information is from State Ed. Their principal arranged for them to be introduced to the Common Core State Standards through a Board of Cooperative Extension representative at a recent faculty meeting. They know everything is in flux: the Common Core State Standards are part of their work-lives now, and word in the pipeline is that state assessments are changing as a result. Today, a representative from State Ed will share more insight and will answer questions. The teachers are happy to hear their request for time in the afternoon to meet with teachers across grade levels to work on curriculum has been acknowledged. They have noted that when students arrive in fourth grade they are not adequately prepared to negotiate the content vocabulary expected of them. The teachers are excited about meeting with the reading specialist regarding this concern. He is going to help them apply to their daily literacy practices what they've been learning about content vocabulary instruction in their collaborative professional learning community the past few months. Each teacher is ready with a list of questions and ideas about which they want to consult with the reading teacher. They are looking forward to articulating their concerns and working with colleagues to problem-solve issues they have noted.

Case Scenario B

PD Day at Cobleskill Elementary

It's yet another professional development day at Cobleskill Elementary. The teachers shuffle into the auditorium armed with papers to grade and mindless paperwork to get done while they are forced to attend this year's district professional development day. The agenda shows they will hear a series of speakers in the morning. The superintendent decided the teachers needed to be informed about the current research in literacy instruction. Her analysis of students' performance on state assessments has shown the district could benefit from focusing on teachers' knowledge of how to effectively teach reading comprehension and vocabulary skills and on writing constructed responses. She is hopeful that after a day of hearing about what scientifically based reading research says about effective methods and strategy instruction, her teachers will integrate new knowledge into their curriculum and daily practices. The teachers are happy that at least they will get the afternoon "off" to work on whatever they want to in their classrooms.

Which professional development day would you rather attend? It's safe to say that as self-motivated educators, we all hope for the kind of day the teachers at Schoharie Elementary are about to experience. Yes? What are the differences between the two scenarios that make Schoharie's day what we crave from a day of professional development?

We note the teachers appear to have had input regarding the agenda for the day. They've recognized particular student needs and have collaborated to set a plan into action for meeting those needs. They have initiated a collaborative professional learning community to study content vocabulary, and they have voiced a request to their administrator for time to work with the reading specialist on applying what they have been learning to their daily practices. The teachers at Cobleskill Elementary are attending a day planned by the superintendent. Apparently, she analyzed students' performance results based on numbers from the state assessments and decided what the teachers needed to learn. This plan follows a very top-down approach that is externally imposed. On the other hand, Schoharie's plan demonstrates a bottom-up approach that is developed internally and locally based on teachers' analyses of students' and their own needs. The agenda seems to have been arrived at in a democratic way.

Fundamentally, the Schoharie professional development day meets these principles of effective professional development identified in current research (Cervetti & Pearson, 2005; Lassonde & Israel, 2010; Pearson, Taylor, & Tam, 2005; Richardson, 2003; Taylor, Pearson, Peterson, & Rodriguez, 2005):

- When teachers feel their beliefs and ideas are valued and recognized, they are more open to new ideas.

- Professional development that fosters continuous learning rather than a "one-shot" remedy is likely to be more effective and long-lasting.

- Opportunities to articulate connections among teacher knowledge, classwork, and standards encourage professional growth and understanding.

- Professional development that helps teachers apply their knowledge and new understandings to particular contexts and students' needs are beneficial.

- When a balance is developed among the students' needs, the school's or program's needs, and the individual teacher's needs, it is more likely teachers will improve their knowledge and skills.

- Concentrated focus on improving in one area is more effective than working on multiple issues at a time.

- Focusing on local context is more likely to succeed than buying into generic approaches.

- Professional development that encourages a collective responsibility for instruction based on shared knowledge and careful analyses of teaching is highly effective and sustainable.

- Collaborative review of data acts as a "safety net" for professional development. Educators are more likely to take risks and work to improve their instructional techniques when they are generating ideas to solve problems related to specific classroom data (Lewis-Spector & Jay, 2011).

The two case scenarios that open this section on professional development illustrate what these principles might look like—or don't—in a district. Does this mean that top-down approaches are bad or wrong and bottom-up approaches are good or right? We don't think so, and we don't want to paint that kind of portrait of professional development.

It might help to think back on the historic "reading wars" of the 1980s and learn from them. On one side of the debate, proponents of meaning-based approaches to teaching reading said instruction should stress comprehension and use good literature to engage children in lots of meaningful reading and writing activities. Basically, children will construct their own meanings with support from teachers and peers through whole-language approaches. On the other side of the debate, proponents of skills-based instruction stated children need direct skills instruction in phonics to read fluently and gain comprehension. Eventually, we have come to know that both approaches are valuable when blended together with scientifically based reading research.

Professional development approaches can be thought of the same way. Can we assume teachers will grow as professionals if we allow them to construct their own plan of growth, their own meanings? Not all teachers know or can easily learn on their own everything they need to know to become the best teachers they can be. The phrase "We don't know what we don't know!" applies here. As the superintendent who planned the professional day for Cobleskill soon found out, attempting to serve up knowledge on a silver platter doesn't necessarily work. It can result in mock compliance or outright rejection of new ideas.

Like with the blended reading approach from the "reading wars" example, we propose teachers need some skills-based direct instruction, or at least direct facilitation, to complement opportunities to construct their own knowledge if they are to develop fully. We aren't saying knowledge should be bound and de-livered; however, teachers benefit from facilitation, modeling, and guided practice, especially when they occur within local contexts, such as classroom spaces. When professional development is interactive, it is likely to build teachers' confidence, strengthen their decision-making abilities, and empower them. Integrating top-down with bottom-up approaches to professional development—as demonstrated by the Schoharie Elementary case scenario—creates a framework to define the expertise to be developed, shape how it is to be implemented, and allow for the flexibility and versatility individual teachers need to achieve expertise (Callahan, Benson-Griffo, & Pearson, 2010). Finally, we like a menu of professional development options so educators and administrators can learn and work together. It is imperative that administrators also keep up to date on effective literacy approaches and programs so they can best facilitate and support educators' and students' progress. In their study of instructional leadership roles for principals, Dowell, Bickmore, and Hoewing (2012) advocate for the adoption of a strong stance that guides both leadership organizations and literacy development. We encourage a PD agenda that allows participants to shift from directed to self-directed activities then back again. This approach allows for differentiation to meet everyone's needs and to position administrators as literacy leaders so they will be prepared to act as knowledgeable mentors and coaches.

The Ethical Literacy Leader feature at the end of this chapter provides insight into how a graduate literacy program seeks to prepare students to meet the professional needs of teachers and students in a particular context while aligning with professional standards. For more insight on how the face of professional development is quickly changing based on funding needs, prepping for the Common Core Standards, and the newest tools technology offers (*Education Week*, 2011), read Chapter 7, Texturizing with Resources.

Painting a Portrait of Literacy-Learning Communities

Many schools are forming professional learning communities (PLCs) to build collaboration among colleagues. These groups may form to facilitate study, research, or inquiry of a topic (Lassonde & Israel, 2010). Here's a perfect example of an effective PLC: In 2004 Sanger Unified school district was identified as one of the 98 lowest-performing school districts in California. By 2008 all seven schools were scoring above the state Academic Performance Index. The district has been hailed as an example of high-capacity systems change. According to the district's superintendent, Marc Johnson, one of the sustained practices attributed to the school's turnaround is the development of PLCs to build collaboration. The district's PLC goals focused on shared decision making, improved technical capacity, release time to support participation in PLCs, and the expectation for cultural change that promoted the sharing of classroom practices and data on a personal level. Sanger Unified's teachers say PLCs provided opportunities for them to analyze data that helped them focus improvement efforts, helped them design effective lessons and assessments to respond to students' needs, and allowed them to experience shared efficacy and accountability by shifting the working culture from one of isolation and competition to one of collaboration. For the full study of the district done by an external research group and more information on PLCs, go to http://www.cacollaborative.org/Meetings/Meeting14PLCs.aspx.

PLCs that focus on literacy are referred to as professional literacy communities or literacy-learning communities (LLCs; Lent, 2007). Here, we will use the latter term to avoid confusing the acronyms PLC and LLC.

Literacy-learning communities, like the Canadian group whose work on the IRIS is described in Case Scenario C, may be initiated within a school district for many purposes (Kanold, 2006). An LLC may present more like a task force that is composed to answer a specific question, such as a group generated for the sole purpose of investigating and deciding which phonics program the district wants to adopt. Or, it may be more long-lasting, such as a study group that meets regularly to share research or participate in a professional book club. LLCs may be initiated or exist to assess a school's literacy needs or to develop a plan for embedded professional development. In the case of in-school LLCs, the participants may be viewed as the literacy leaders of the school sheerly by their membership in the group. Or, there may be a person they have identified as the school's literacy leader who facilitates the group's meetings. The project team that created the IRIS situated assessment acted as literacy leaders by informing the district's reform movement, collecting and analyzing data, theorizing collaboratively, sharing their results with teacher leaders from each school, and supporting the district's progress.

The roles of the literacy leader in an LLC may be to build and nurture relationships within the group, provide resources and expertise, and mentor members to become literacy leaders for their building. We like the idea of having group members share the role of leader or take turns in the leadership role. This approach encourages everyone to engage in leadership and brings out fresh ideas. By using critical inquiry to address their students' reading comprehension needs and relegating power to key leaders within individual schools within their district, the

Case Scenario C

An Effective Literacy-Learning Community

When three university professors and five mentor teachers came together to work out a way to improve reading comprehension in Grades 4 through 8 in a school in western Canada, they formed an LLC that would help to reform their district. The LLC members chose to develop their project around reading comprehension strategies that would help students make connections, engage with texts, construct meaning, monitor their understanding, analyze and synthesize information, and develop critical reading strategies. Their project involved exploring the use of a "situated assessment," which they define as "an assessment tool that is collaboratively developed and used in the context of a particular reform effort and is meant to benefit teachers who use it by informing their instruction" (Rogers et al., 2006, p. 544). The sole purpose of the situated assessment was for use as a professional development tool; the group developed the Informal Reading Inventory of Strategies (IRIS) to support and enhance the goals of the project team (see Rogers et al., 2006).

group in Case Scenario C portrayed multiple leadership roles. Key processes that maintain LLCs include the following:

- Begin by discussing the group's literacy goals.
- Negotiate the goals if diverse ideas exist.
- Engage in professional, respectful conversations about teaching literacy.
- Come to the meetings prepared.
- Choose a convenient setting and time and maintain a flexible routine (Goatley, 2010).

For more information about initiating and sustaining professional collaborative communities, we like *Teacher Collaboration for Professional Learning: Facilitating Study, Research, and Inquiry Communities* (Lassonde & Israel, 2010). Also, see this chapter's Critical Voices feature wherein Katie Stover talks about her school's collaborative efforts.

Literacy-learning communities also exist outside of a school building or district. For example, Virginia Goatley, the research director of the International Reading Association, in her article "Finding a Voice in Professional Literacy Communities" (2011), views these communities as a "range of professional communities of educators" (p. 16). She proposes we all can be literacy leaders by voicing our opinions and providing feedback on state or national policies and initiatives. Our classrooms are influenced by the standards, frameworks, and policies being implemented, so we not only have the *right* to speak out but it is our *responsibility* to speak out about educational policy and reform. (See this chapter's The Ethical Literacy Leader for an example of how standards influence Deborah Bordelon's teaching. Also, read more about external forms of LLCs and networking in Chapter 7, Texturizing with Resources.)

Closing Thoughts

Literacy leaders are empowered to envision a dream of what literacy leadership looks like in a school district and then paint it, as Van Gogh's quote at the beginning of this chapter implies. By reflecting on and applying the information about goals, effective professional development, and literacy-learning communities shared in this chapter, you can begin to paint the literacy program that will best serve the students, educators, families, and communities in your district.

Next, we invite you to hear the voices of literacy leaders in the field as you read and contemplate The Ethical Literacy Leader and Critical Voices features in this chapter. Following each feature are questions in the Cultivate Your Leadership Skills section to prompt your thinking as you work toward painting a vision of literacy leadership in your context. To read more about the contributors' backgrounds, see the About the Contributors section.

The Ethical Literacy Leader

Complementing Professional Standards with Personal Standards

—DEBORAH BORDELON

Deborah currently serves as dean of the College of Education and dean of Graduate Studies at Governors State University in Illinois. She was also the cochair for the International Reading Association's Professional Standards and Ethics Committee for 2011–2012.

As university professors, my colleagues and I prepare literacy leaders who will fill positions in school districts as reading specialists and literacy coaches. Ultimately, we want educators to exit our graduate programs knowing how to effectively serve their schools and districts. It is our responsibility—with the guidance of the Standards for Reading Professionals (International Reading Association [IRA], 2010)— to determine how to provide the knowledge and the appropriate classroom experiences graduates need to succeed. We think of this as complementing the professional standards with our personal set of standards and goals for our graduates. We have found the key to understanding our roles as ethical literacy leaders is in recognizing that graduates exit our programs as novice coaches and then need to continue their learning journey. They will continue to develop as effective leaders as they take on responsibilities and interact with teachers at the school and district levels through professional activities. We aim to prepare our graduates for this ultimate challenge.

The Standards for Reading Professionals (IRA, 2010) to which we referred previously outline the professional expectations for literacy coaches and reading specialists. Professional standards ensure there is consistency in preparation and expectations are clearly defined. They provide the metric by which programs may be judged. Therefore, our programs must clearly align with the standards; and we have to demonstrate how graduates of the programs are able to demonstrate mastery of the standards. However, how a teacher education program chooses to address the standards may vary depending upon its mission, conceptual framework, geographic location, and other variables.

Beyond the standards, as educators we know the reality of the demands of literacy leaders in the field. We recognize the importance of graduates of our programs knowing how to meet the particular needs of their districts. Furthermore, we know literacy coaching requires a different set of skills and dispositions from teaching. The focus is on adult learning as opposed to student learning, so many teachers must shift their perspectives and pedagogically appropriate instructional strategies. Reading specialists and literacy coaches need to have the knowledge and skills to support struggling readers, but they also need to be prepared to step into the role of assisting teachers, often their own colleagues. This may take place in learning communities, workshops, classroom observations, and modeling. In addition, the reading specialist may be required to provide the leadership and informed knowledge for the implementation of reading programs to a school or district.

To help our graduates succeed in meeting the various expectations they may face in their districts or positions, we integrate a continuum of coaching experiences that will adequately prepare a reading specialist or literacy coach to enter into a leadership role. This typically involves field experiences at the university, school, and district levels. How that continuum is structured, implemented, and assessed is guided by the professional standards, but must be determined by the program. This leaves the program with the interesting challenge to prepare these prospective leaders to understand the importance of developing and implementing quality professional development for teachers and other staff who will have an impact on the literacy education of students.

Our university continually reflects on ethical decisions that shape how we prepare our graduates. We know there isn't one right way to implement the professional standards. We also know we have an ethical duty to meet what the profession has determined to be the appropriate level of knowledge, skills, and professional dispositions with what the program faculty, students, and community members have identified as their needs. Collectively, my colleagues, guided by the IRA Professional Standards, capitalize on the opportunities and address the challenges of effectively preparing literacy leaders to lead professional development efforts that will positively impact teachers and students.

Cultivate Your Leadership Skills

1. How do Deborah and her colleagues seek to help their graduates meet the three goals of literacy leaders outlined in this chapter?
2. How do Deborah and her colleagues as literacy leaders themselves meet the three goals of literacy leaders outlined in this chapter?
3. Deborah and her colleagues want to prepare graduates to know how to meet the needs of diverse communities. How might they prepare graduates to work as literacy leaders at the two school districts described in Case Scenarios A and B in this chapter?

Critical Voices

Chipping Away at a Wall of Resistance

—KATIE STOVER

Katie is a former elementary teacher and literacy coach. Currently, she is an assistant professor at Furman University in Greenville, South Carolina.

Painting my dream of working as a literacy coach was mirrored after the relationship I had with the literacy coach at my school when I was a fourth-grade teacher. This coach, Karen, spent countless hours in my classroom modeling effective teaching practices, meeting with me individually to discuss my questions and challenges, and keeping me abreast of the latest trends in literacy research and practice through professional development. She inspired my dream of becoming a literacy coach through the impact she made on my abilities to teach effectively and enhance my knowledge. I was thrilled when I was asked to move into the role of the literacy coach to paint my dream. I was eager to work with other teachers, share my knowledge and passion for learning, and inspire other teachers to continue to grow professionally.

Based on my job description and the needs of the school, I wore many hats as a literacy coach and had numerous responsibilities: I organized and maintained a book room where teachers checked out materials; I provided small-group intervention instruction; and I met with teachers on a regular basis to provide ongoing support and professional development. Much of my role was spent working with teachers to foster ongoing differentiated support to develop their knowledge, skills, and dispositions (Stover, Kissel, Haag, & Shoniker, 2011). I knew that to successfully work with these teachers, I would first need to establish a rapport with each individual teacher and develop trusting relationships (L'Allier, Elish-Piper, & Bean, 2010).

Unfortunately, however, initially some of the teachers were resistant to change and to working collaboratively. I did not receive the warm welcome I was expecting. Many teachers simply avoided me while others explicitly stated they had taught for more than 20 years (emphasizing they had more teaching experience than I had) and did not need additional support.

In an effort to begin to chip away at the walls the teachers created in an attempt to avoid change, I needed to get to know each teacher individually and foster a sense of community and collaboration. Not only was it crucial that I establish relationships with each teacher, but to shift from the previous paradigm of skill-and-drill, scripted instruction and practice, I first had to get teacher buy-in. Knowing that it was going to be difficult to gain the trust of the teachers and be welcomed into their classrooms based on their avoidance and resistance to change, it was essential for me to build relationships.

Taking time to get to know the teachers on an individual basis both personally and professionally showed the teachers that I cared about them as individuals. I found any reason to visit their classrooms and increase my presence. For example, I offered to visit their classrooms in nonthreatening ways by asking if I could read to their classes, help organize their classroom libraries, and do individualized assessments with students who seemed to be struggling. After increasing my presence in their classrooms, I began to work more directly with the teachers by offering to model strategies with demonstration lessons, share sample lesson ideas, and provide resources. I used the demonstration lessons as a way to begin to gain access to the teachers by meeting with them to debrief after the lesson.

During this time together, we discussed what was working as well as their goals moving forward. I gradually developed rapport and gained the trust of the teachers through my increased involvement as a collaborator in their classrooms. I was transparent about my role as nonevaluative but supportive to help enhance teachers' instruction, analyze data, and improve students' academic success (Shanklin, 2007). When teachers began to realize that I was not there to evaluate them or report back to administration, they began to trust me and slowly began asking for my assistance. Slowly, I gained the teachers' trust and was able to chip away at their walls of resistance and develop a professional collaborative community. Together, we worked to introduce progressive methods that were meaningful and beneficial to students' learning. Eventually, I became the literacy leader I had admired in my mentor, Karen.

While I am no longer a literacy facilitator at this school, I continue to maintain strong, trustful working relationships with many of the teachers I supported. We discuss current trends in literacy instruction and research; I participate in their professional book clubs; and many hosted preservice teachers from the courses I taught at the University of North Carolina at Charlotte. Many teachers also invite me into their classrooms and share the various instructional strategies and happenings in their classrooms. These ongoing collegial relationships demonstrate the power of

building rapport and developing a sense of collaboration to foster professional growth and enhance student learning.

Cultivate Your Leadership Skills

1. What characteristics did Katie and Mr. DeVitto have in common as literacy leaders? See Mr. DeVitto's story in the Goal #3: Literacy Leaders Seek to Affect School Culture section of this chapter.

2. This chapter offers many suggestions for painting a vision of LLCs. Katie expresses having tried several of them. What other suggestions from this chapter would have helped Katie develop a collaborative literacy community?

3. How might Katie have empowered the teachers with whom she was working? How might mutual feelings of empowerment have fostered the development of the LLC?

Questions for Reflection and Discussion

1. Review the complete definition of professional development as delineated in the Elementary and Secondary Education Act at http://www2.ed.gov/policy/elsec/leg/esea02/pg107.html. How does the research cited in this chapter align with the Act's description of activities that fit its definition? What does this tell you about the formation of this government policy?

2. Discuss the various types of professional development in which you have participated. Which forms were more or less beneficial

for you? How do the kinds of professional development you experienced align with the characteristics identified in this chapter?

3. Discuss the various types of professional learning communities with which you have participated. Which were more or less beneficial for you and why?

4. Referring to the beginning quote from Van Gogh, how would you "paint your dream" for literacy leadership to fit the context of your school, students, and community?

Practical Applications

How might this chapter apply to your teaching context and experience? Try these activities:

Classroom Activity

After engaging in some form of literacy professional development, such as attending a conference or participating in a think tank with colleagues, try out some of the new methods or ideas you heard about. Share with a colleague what you tried and how it worked. Do you think the professional development was effective based on your classroom application results? Why or why not?

Professional Development Activity

Collaborate with colleagues to organize some type of professional development to promote the enhancement of literacy leadership at your grade level, in your school, or in your district.

Consider initiating a study group, workshop, faculty presentation, or some other form of professional development to work toward one of the three goals for literacy leaders described in this chapter.

Here's another idea: Faculty meetings are a powerful venue for professional development. Coaches are encouraged to ask school administrators if they can be afforded time to present at faculty meetings. As all faculty and staff are usually present, this is a perfect opportunity to share information and celebrate success while advertising the value of a shared vision and commitment to life-long learning and job-embedded professional development. Consistent use of time across all faculty meetings creates the expectation that we will study an aspect of literacy together and sends the message that literacy and professional learning are important.

References

Barcott, R. (2011). *It happened on the way to war: A marine's path to peace.* New York: Bloomsbury.

Callahan, M., Benson-Griffo, V., & Pearson, P. D. (2010). Teacher knowledge and teaching reading. In W. M. Linek, D. D. Massey, L. Cochran, E. G. Sturtevant, B. McClanahan, & M. B. Sampson (Eds.), *College Reading Association legacy: A celebration of 50 years of literacy leadership, volume II* (pp. 947–970). Association of Literacy Educators and Researchers.

Cervetti, G., & Pearson, P. D. (2005). A model of professional growth in reading education. In C. Snow, M. Griffin, & S. Burns (Eds.), *Knowledge to support the teaching of reading: Preparing teachers for a changing world* (pp. 201–224). San Francisco: Jossey-Bass.

Davis, E. E. (Ed.) (2006). *Qualities for effective leadership: School leaders speak.* Lanham, MD: Rowman & Littlefield Education.

Dowell, S., Bickmore, D., & Hoewing, B. (2012). A framework for defining literacy leadership. *Journal of Reading Education, 37*(2), 7–15.

DuFour, R., DuFour, R., & Eaker, R. (2008). *Revisiting professional learning communities at work: New insights for improving schools.* Bloomington, IN: Solution Tree Press.

Education Week. (2011). Virtual PD creates connections. Retrieved from http:// www.edweek. org/go/elearningPD

George, P., & Aronson, R. (n.d.). *How do educators' cultural belief systems affect underserved students' pursuit of postsecondary education?* Honolulu, HI: Pacific Resources for Education and Learning. Available online at http://www .prel.org/products/pn_/cultural-belief.htm.

Goatley, G. (2010). Thinking together: Creating and sustaining professional learning communities. In C. Lassonde & S. E. Israel (Eds.), *Teacher collaboration for professional learning: Facilitating study, research, and inquiry communities.* San Francisco: Jossey-Bass.

Goatley, V. (2011). Finding a voice in professional literacy communities. *Reading Today, 29*(1), 16–17.

International Reading Association. (2010). *Standards for reading professionals.* Newark, DE: Author.

Johnson, K. E. (1992). The relationship between teachers' beliefs and practices during literacy instruction for non-native speakers of English. *Journal of Reading Behavior, 24*(1), 83–108.

Kanold, T. (2006). The continuous improvement wheel of a professional learning community. *Journal of Staff Development, 27*(2), 16–21.

Kuzborska, I. (2011). Links between teachers' beliefs and practices and research on reading. *Reading in a Foreign Language, 23*(1), 102–128.

L'Allier, S., Elish-Piper, L., & Bean, R. (2010). What matters for elementary literacy coaching? Guiding principles for instructional improvement and student achievement. *Reading Teacher, 63*(7), 544–554.

Lassonde, C. A., & Israel, S. E. (2010). *Teacher collaboration for professional learning:* *Facilitating study, research, and inquiry communities.* San Francisco: Jossey-Bass.

Lent, R. C. (2007). *Literacy-learning communities.* Portsmouth, NH: Heinemann.

Lewis-Spector, J., & Jay, A. B. (2011). *Leadership for literacy in the 21st century.* Association of Literacy Educators and Researchers White Paper.

McLesky, J., & Waldron, N. L. (2011). Educational programs for elementary students with learning disabilities: Can they be both effective and inclusive? *Learning Disabilities Research & Practice, 26*(1), 46–57.

Meltzer, J., & Hamann, E. T. (2005). *Meeting the literacy development needs of adolescent English-language learners through content-area learning: Part two: Focus on classroom teaching and learning strategies.* Providence, RI: The Education Alliance at Brown University. Retrieved from http://www.alliance. brown.edu/pubs/adlit/adell_litdv1.pdf

National Staff Development Council. (n.d.).Retrieved from http://www.learningforward.org/standfor/definition.cfm

Pearson, P. D., Taylor, B. M., & Tam, A. (2005). Effective professional development for improving literacy instruction. In R. Indrisano & J. R. Paratore (Eds.), *Learning to write, writing to learn: Research and theory in practice* (pp. 221–224). Newark, DE: International Reading Association.

Richardson, V. (2003). The dilemmas of professional development. *Phi Delta Kappan, 84*(5), 401–406.

Rogers, T., Winters, K. L., Bryan, G., Price, J., McCormick, F., House, L., Mezzarobba, D., & Sinclaire,C. (2006). Developing the IRIS: Toward situated and valid assessment measures in collaborative professional development and school reform in literacy. *Reading Teacher, 59*(6.4), 544–553.

Shanklin, N. L. (2007). What supports do literacy coaches need from administrators in order to succeed? Literacy Coaching Clearinghouse. Retrieved from http://www.literacycoachinonline.org/briefs/LCSupportsNSBrief.pdf

Stover, K., Kissel, B., Haag, K., & Shoniker, R. (2011). Differentiated coaching: Fostering reflection with teachers. *Reading Teacher, 64*(7), 498–509.

Taylor, B. M., Pearson, P. D., Peterson, D. S., & Rodriguez, M. C. (2005). The CIERA school change framework: An evidence-based approach to professional development and school reading improvement. *Reading Research Quarterly, 40*(1), 40–69.

Woolfolk Hoy, A., Davis, H., & Pape, S. (2006). Teachers' knowledge, beliefs, and thinking. In P. A. Alexander & P. H. Winne (Eds.), *Handbook of educational psychology* (2nd ed., pp. 715–737). Mahwah, NJ: Erlbaum.

Nurturing a Mosaic of Adult Learners

> ❝ *The point is to know how to use the colours, the choice of which is, when all's said and done, a matter of habit.* ❞
>
> —CLAUDE MONET

Introduction

In the opening quote, Monet describes how a painting as a whole is made up of a mosaic of colors. This quote might also suggest that each color is unique and offers something special to the picture. In this chapter, we look at the relationship between literacy leadership and adult learning in similar ways: as a means to weave together a strong literacy community that to the indiscreet eye is a "matter of habit" and as a manner to recognize the individual colors each person offers the painting or literacy-learning community.

Adult learning, in the form of teaching educators, is at the heart of literacy leadership. To design relevant, motivating, and ultimately differentiated professional development honoring adult learners, literacy leaders need to embrace, understand, and live the principles of adult education. This chapter provides six principles of adult learning as applied to literacy leadership. These six principles serve literacy leaders best when embraced as a philosophy and used as the "why" in designing professional development for adult learners. They recognize adult learners as a mosaic of colors that build a seamless literacy-learning community while recognizing, as Monet proposes, the individual contributions each member offers. (Read this chapter's The Common Core State Standards Connection by Tracey Johnson for thoughts about preparing for change.)

Working with a Mosaic of Adult Learners

As enthusiastic as literacy leaders may be to dive straight into the "what" and "how" of designing professional development activities for adults, leaders should first delve into the underlying "why" that actually drives adult learning. It is critical that we embrace a philosophy of adult education and its mission to nurture lifelong learning, for this is what helps us stay the course during our tenure as literacy leaders. Literacy leaders can draw from andragogy, the art and science of adult education, to sculpt a philosophy that will guide us in the why, what, and how involved in leading others with compassion and integrity. See Dawn Hamlin's Response to Intervention (RTI) and the Literacy Leader feature for an example of the value of effective adult education and training.

While literacy leadership includes delivering content in the form of reading, writing, and classroom management strategies, leaders must also weave in the process of adult learning, focusing on how a group of diverse adults learns best. When we consider how adults learn best and follow through by creating learning experiences based on these principles, we are truly differentiating our instruction

The Common Core State Standards Connection
Preparing for the Journey Ahead
—TRACEY JOHNSON

Tracey's career in education spans over 22 years. She has taught at all educational levels, developed curriculum, provided professional development to persistently low-achieving schools, and mentored teachers. She is currently employed at the New York State Education Department.

The prologue of a story sets the context for the reader. This roadmap gives the reader a precursor for what has to be considered before taking the ride. The details included in this section of the text provide a stream of consciousness for the journey ahead. This is the case with the "Introduction" of the Common Core State Standards. In this roadmap we find out that before one can plow full speed ahead toward implementing the standards, there must be cogitation for the complexity of putting these standards into practice.

It is in the Introduction that we find out what the standards are and what they are not. They are not curriculum; they are not lesson plans; and they do not define intervention methods or materials. While on this journey of Common Core implementation, teachers are expected to use their professional knowledge and judgment to determine appropriate tools and knowledge that students will need to meet the goals as established by the Common Core State Standards, thus creating a freedom of creativity and independence. For example, teachers, curriculum developers, and states may determine a particular writing process or a full range of metacognitive strategies that students may need to monitor and direct their thinking and learning. Additionally, Appendices A, B, and C provide supplemental resources, such as a glossary, recommendations for exemplary text selections, and student writing samples.

Response to Intervention (RTI) and the Literacy Leader
Training for the Data Olympics
—DAWN HAMLIN

Dawn is a former special education teacher who taught in both traditional public schools and residential facilities. Currently, she is assistant professor in the Educational Psychology Department at SUNY College at Oneonta.

Welcome to the Data Olympics—otherwise known as RTI! Relevant data are imperative for literacy leaders in regard to making good evidence-based instructional and intervention decisions. This data collection process would be overwhelming for a single RTI team member;

however, a good literacy leader will help to provide training and assist with the many "events" that make RTI sometimes feel like a new Olympic game.

In many classrooms today there are often several educational team members involved in various activities with the students. The classroom setting often includes the general education teacher, special education teacher, paraprofessionals, and perhaps a speech-language specialist or behavior therapist. Each of these potential RTI team members can play a valuable role in the data collection process; however, for many, data collection is a new frontier.

The literacy leader should plan and develop training modules that will help these key team players score big in Data Olympic events such as the Curriculum-Based Measurement (CBM) Marathon (or how to create and score the CBM), the Daily Data Speed Trials (aka oral reading fluency measures such as repeated reading), the 5K (or 3K or 6K—you get the picture), Graph Climb (otherwise known as graphing results for five or more students), and the Final Evaluation Event where critical instructional decisions are made.

Without careful planning and effective training, data may indeed be collected, but whether or not it is of any instructional use will be questionable. Continued training for adult learners on key data collection procedures will help maintain procedural fidelity and help with efficiency and efficacy in the classroom.

The final results of great Data Olympic training should be targeted data that will help instructors adjust interventions, instruction, or goals so our students make appropriate academic progress and successfully meet their desired goals.

while honoring the diverse talents of adult learners. Honoring adult learners is the spirit of literacy leadership.

There are six assumptions (Knowles, Holton, & Swanson, 2011) at the heart of adult education that can help literacy leaders plan effective professional growth. These assumptions can serve literacy leaders well when they are embraced as principles of literacy leadership. These principles help literacy leaders understand why learning conditions and learning experiences are set up in certain ways for those adults participating in job-embedded professional development. Leaders will come to realize why high-quality professional development cannot be a "one-size-fits-all" approach. Those who are in the business of educating adults understand and embrace the following assumptions:

1. Adult learners need to know why they are being asked to learn something new, before engaging in the learning process.
2. Adult learners come to learning situations with a wealth of experience.
3. Adults are ready to learn when they perceive the need to change to be more effective at what they do.
4. Adults are motivated to learn after they experience the need for a change.
5. Adults are motivated to learn based on internal needs.
6. Adult learners are self-directing.

In considering these six understandings, it is easy to see that adults are coming to the "painting"—the literacy community—with varied identities, interests, values, beliefs, experiences, and preconceived philosophies about reading, writing, and classroom management.

Imagine that you are suddenly told that you must comply with a new district initiative, a top-down mandate that changes the way you have been teaching reading or writing for 3, 5, 10, 15, or 20 years. How would you feel, react, and respond to the mandate? What view will you have of the situation and relationship? Will you take charge of your own learning within the relationship? Do you think it will be easy to change? Do you think it will be easy for everyone around you to change? With the six assumptions previously identified, literacy leaders can plan and facilitate professional development activities with adult learners fully in mind. Let's take a closer look at each principle to consider how it directly applies to literacy leadership.

Assumption #1: Adult learners need to know why they are being asked to learn something new, before engaging in the learning process.

The essence of this principle is quite simple in that teachers affected by curricular changes desire to know ahead of time the reasons for having to learn something new, and the reasons why they will need to learn new information.

What is it, then, that this principle calls for in practice? It calls for leaders to be sensitive to time and rationale. Teachers have a right to know what is coming and why in a timely manner. Time and rationale offer teachers the chance to accept the initial idea that something is going to change, that they are about to learn something new. It offers an open window to preparedness, allowing teachers to get their minds ready to learn. "Ahead of time" may have diverse connotations for different people. It would be wise for the leader to learn about individual teachers' sense of time. Does "ahead of time" mean a year, months, weeks, days, hours, minutes? If a leader can tap into a teacher's value on time and preparedness, the leader is demonstrating a high degree of respect for the learner and therefore cultivating a positive leading relationship—one built on respect.

Literacy leaders need to keep in mind that time and rationale run through the very fabric of leading in all situations. Using the following ideas may jump-start proactive practices and relationships or may help get them back on track.

- Work with administrators advocating that teachers be included in conversations about new initiatives and change expectations, before the change occurs. This consideration is accomplished during faculty meetings and then nurtured through letters to the staff, e-mail, and one-to-one conversations. If faculty meetings are not an option, then utilize committees or other small-group scenarios.

- Meet with individual teachers prior to cycles of professional development to have conversations about their reactions, feelings, beliefs, and ideas in relation to the new initiative. If possible, offer some information ahead of time to help alleviate anxieties. Answer questions. Listen attentively to concerns. Express sincere concern.

- Gently alert teachers of upcoming workshops, meetings, group work, and so forth through letters or e-mail using a personal touch. Memos can sometimes come across as sterile and unfriendly. Remember, teachers are people first, then partners in the literacy relationship. People deserve to be treated with care.

For each learning experience or activity, have an agenda written ahead of time. Send the agenda out prior to the learning experience to engender preparedness and rationale. Adults will come to the activity prepared, knowing what to expect. Having a written agenda helps guide the learning experience and keeps everyone on track, including the leader. Explain the agenda at the start of the learning experience in ways that position it as framework for thinking and working, a framework that can be renegotiated as needed to promote group learning and to achieve the goals of the inquiry work itself. Use the agenda during the experience to stay on track. Go over the agenda at the closing to celebrate all that was accomplished. This creates a climate of success by negotiating goals as a team. Collaboratively design the next agenda.

Assumption #2: Adult learners come to learning situations with a wealth of experience.

Effective literacy leaders value this reality and embrace all that it offers. Individuals within any group come with diverse experiences, values, interests, and beliefs. When leaders celebrate diversity and nurture the sharing of knowledge and experience, a climate of trust emerges and relationships are enriched. People have a right to be and feel valued. People also have a right to discuss their views freely in proactive ways, for or even against initiatives. Leaders need to be prepared for this level of thinking and facilitating.

Think of a time when you were expected to learn something new. Was it a risk-free environment? Were you able to speak freely? Ask questions? Agree or disagree? Did you feel valued? Imagine working in an environment where you are not valued. Would change in your practice occur wholeheartedly? Literacy leaders can engender this respect for personal experience and background knowledge by doing the following:

- Intentionally make room in conversations and learning activities for other people's opinions, personal experiences, and divergent thinking.

- Create surveys to find out what teachers know and use as part of their current teaching repertoire, what they value, how they perceive a particular practice or issue, and where they believe their skills lie in relation to the practice or issue. Integrate the information gleaned from these surveys to enrich literacy- and teaching-learning experiences and to create a culture of respect and lifelong learning.

■ Nurture natural leadership abilities in teachers by asking them to share their expertise. Teachers should be encouraged to share information or present information more formally to small and large groups. Teachers should also be encouraged to open their classrooms for others to visit, observing literacy in action. During the visits teachers can model literacy practices based on their own areas of strength and expertise.

Assumption #3: Adults are ready to learn when they perceive the need to change to be more effective at what they do.

This principle brings to light another timing issue for literacy leaders and teachers. With this assumption in mind, literacy leaders need to understand and value the adage that "timing is everything." Adults are ready to learn when they recognize their own need to make a change. This recognition comes through reflection and will be different for everyone in terms of the type of change and also the timing of the change. In essence, teachers are in the driver's seat when it comes to readiness to learn (see Barth, 1990).

Oftentimes, leaders are asked to work with a variety of teachers, some of whom are always ready and eager to learn, others who are ready to learn under specific circumstances, and those who are not ready to learn. This principle is quite important for literacy leaders to adopt as part of their practice. Literacy leaders need to prioritize and allocate their time effectively to work with many colleagues and students. It is wise to begin by spending much more time with those who are ready and willing. In doing so, the leader is building school capacity, nurturing and empowering teacher leaders, and creating a support system for other teachers to utilize as they are ready. While this is occurring, the literacy leader continues to build and maintain relationships with all teachers, even those reluctant to fully engage. (Read this chapter's Critical Voices feature to see how critically important it is to build and maintain respectful relationships in a community of learners.)

When literacy leaders are proactive and patient, even the most reluctant teachers emerge ready to learn in time. What can a leader do to encourage and nurture readiness to learn? A few possible suggestions are the following:

■ Openly discuss the nature of professional development, use democratic processes, and advocate that professional development be voluntary. This method is proactive and allows the leader to build capacity with those who are ready, while building up relationships and readiness with others.

- Create plenty of opportunity for reflection. Reflection helps teachers think about what they already know and do against a benchmark for new learning. It is in the mismatch or space between present levels of performance, interests, beliefs, values, or attitudes and the new learning benchmark where a need to learn may be identified. After teachers have observed a model lesson or video, visited a classroom or school, or engaged in some other learning activity, the leader should provide time for reflection and conversation. The enthusiasm to learn emanating from one teacher may in fact encourage or spark the readiness to learn in someone else.

- Plan differentiated cycles of professional development. Literacy leaders can use surveys to assess teacher interests. Once the information is gathered, leaders can plan for book clubs, courses, visitations and observations, or workshops on select topics. Teachers can sign up voluntarily to be a part of the group. Therefore, the learning is much more grassroots and low risk than other modes of professional development. This process may move teachers toward readiness, especially in a climate where timing is valued.

- Celebrate teachers in the process of learning! Advertise success through e-mails, newsletters, teacher of the week, toasts at faculty meetings, notes and banners in the teachers' room, and so forth. Leaders can create the climate to celebrate the small steps forward, and maybe this too can affect readiness.

Assumption #4: Adults are motivated to learn after they experience the need for a change.

Once the need for change is experienced and realized, teachers are motivated to engage in the learning process, and therefore change their practice toward effective literacy instruction. This principle indicates that something has happened to the teacher for him or her to realize that a shift in practice is needed. What sparks such a transition toward motivation for learning? How might a literacy leader nurture transition periods? Let's consider four scenarios.

Each of these case scenarios demonstrates how a teacher can be affected by an experience and then motivated to learn. It is also easy to see how literacy leaders take on certain roles or identities and use particular strategies because they know their learners. (See Chapter 6 for more information about literacy-leadership strategies.) Although each scenario is based on a different leader as actor, effective leaders negotiate their identities when working with diverse teachers, in diverse situations. Therefore, it is so important for literacy leaders to have many response options available when nurturing teachers into and through the learning zone. (Read this chapter's The Ethical Literacy Leader to see how Mary Ann's role as a literacy leader has been changed based on current educational policies.)

Case Scenario A

Joyce is an eighth-grade language arts teacher, someone highly respected and with many years of experience. Joyce has just returned from a literacy institute where she learned about reading workshop and the effect this method of instruction can have on readers and reading achievement. Joyce has always prided herself on the way she runs literature circles but feels ready for a change. Feeling invigorated from so much learning of her own, and realizing the effect this model can have on students, Joyce bought her own resources and began planning to make this change in her practice. Joyce ran into the literacy leader in their school building. Joyce shared her enthusiasm and growing knowledge about reading workshop. Seeing a wonderful opportunity to collaborate, the literacy leader asked if Joyce would be interested in coteaching reading workshop so they could both learn more together. Joyce agreed.

Joyce had a positive learning experience during the week-long institute she attended, returning to her own school highly motivated to make changes. The literacy leader listened as Joyce shared what she had learned and her plan. The literacy leader sensed an opening and asked if Joyce would like to coteach, to work together to build the reading workshop model. This coteaching will be a learning experience for Joyce and the literacy leader. Had Joyce declined the offer, the literacy leader would have supported her change efforts in other ways.

Case Scenario B

Beth is new to teaching third grade; she has taught kindergarten and first grade for several years. Beth recently met with her grade-level colleagues to discuss standardized testing and the current writing curriculum. Beth was startled to realize that all of her third-grade colleagues use writing workshop to deliver differentiated instruction. Beth reflected upon what she used when teaching kindergarten and first-grade students, comparing it to what these third-grade teachers were explaining. Beth felt pressured, as she was the only one in the group who did not know writing workshop, plus she was new to third grade. Beth decided to solicit the assistance of the literacy leader.

The sharing of information, reflection, and personal affect in feeling inadequate is what Beth experienced. This experience motivated Beth to learn more about writing workshop to increase her knowledge in relation to her grade-level colleagues, improve her self-esteem in regard to feeling inadequate, and improve her effectiveness. When Beth contacts the literacy leader, the literacy leader should make himself or herself available and ready to listen to Beth as she shares her current concerns and needs. The literacy leader will be able to offer resources and demonstration lessons right away.

Case Scenario C

Bob is a high school English teacher. He is busy scoring quarterly writing assessments and comes to realize that his class did not perform as well as he had hoped. Although the literacy leader does not work with Bob, she pops her head into his room to say hello and sees Bob with a disappointed look on his face. With genuine care and concern, she encourages Bob to share what he is working on, and he does. By asking reflective questions, the literacy leader helps Bob reflect and figure out for himself what he would like to do. She has not told him what to do, nor made any suggestions. She has given him an opportunity to reflect on his students' work and his teaching methods. Bob shares that he would be interested in learning more about how to teach essay writing. The literacy leader offers to share a list of essay writing strategies and states that she is available to model demonstration lessons if he is interested. Bob agrees to both.

In this scenario, Bob is scoring essays and faced with the lack of progress his students are making in writing. This experience has motivated him to continue learning about essay writing. The literacy leader did not stop by Bob's classroom by chance. As part of her literacy-leadership role and practice, she quickly visits teachers across grade levels to simply say hello, with no strings attached. Timing was perfect today, as it turned out that Bob did, in fact, need assistance. The literacy leader used questioning techniques to help Bob figure out for himself what he'd like to do about his situation. This is gentle leading and an important step in their collaborative relationship.

Case Scenario D

Trish just left the principal's office, her yearly evaluation forms in hand. The principal, knowledgeable in literacy practices, observed a writing workshop session that Trish led for her fifth-grade students. He had questions and concerns regarding what he observed. The principal directed Trish to meet with the literacy leader to work on conferring with students during the writing workshop. Reluctantly, Trish contacted the literacy leader and asked to meet to discuss the delivery of minilessons.

During their conversation, Trish explained what had occurred and her perceptions. The literacy leader listened carefully and recognized Trish was feeling undervalued and unmotivated to learn. In response, the literacy leader wanted to empower Trish to make her own choices in line with the principal's directive. He offered Trish time to plan lessons together, model demonstration lessons, and observe minilessons in a variety of classrooms across the grades.

Trish chose to observe minilessons in action across the grades, then to plan lessons with the literacy leader.

In this instance, Trish went through a negative experience whereby she was directed by her principal to visit with the leader to improve her performance. While such directives are usually counterproductive and build resentment, the literacy leader was able to empower Trish as much as possible by offering choice in how to learn.

Assumption #5: Adults are motivated to learn based on internal needs.

We have seen how motivation is critical to adult learning as it ignites the learning process, but it can also keep the learning moving forward. Adults are motivated through their personal desires to increase self-esteem, gain recognition, shift quality of life, find improved self-confidence, and self-actualize. With this being the case, literacy leaders must set up quality learning experiences or situations where teachers authentically experience self-esteem, receive consistent recognition for their learning efforts and success, and engage in reflection often enough to be able to notice positive changes in themselves. Motivation is not ignited just because an authority figure initiates a change. Teachers must have something to gain that is highly valuable and highly personal. The exchange needs to be mutually enhancing.

Think back to Case Scenario D involving Trish. Her principal directed her to see the literacy leader to work on minilessons. This directive caused Trish to contact the literacy lead, but did not motivate her to want to learn, nor actually learn. Perhaps Trish's motivation to learn will blossom as she chooses her own learning trajectory and as she realizes the impact improved performance will have on her quality of work and self-esteem.

What else can literacy leaders do to tap into teachers' internal reward system?

- Create a survey to learn what motivates teachers. Use the information throughout professional learning activities to connect motivation with the implementation of new practices.
- Give kudos! Advertise the gems! Celebrate! Publish a weekly or monthly literacy-leadership newsletter to celebrate teachers' risk taking, learning journeys, and new practices. If not a leading newsletter, write up a paragraph for an existing newsletter. The key here is to advertise success. This creates fuel for learning.

- Use the art of communication in genuine ways. Listen well to figure out what the teacher is really saying he or she needs. Offer praise at the right time, in the right amount, tapping into a teacher's sense of self. Seek to empower teachers using choice words. Diffuse negative situations by listening well and offering viable alternatives. Use reflective questions to help teachers choose for themselves what they want or need.

- Ask teachers to describe a time when their own adult learning was a success. What was special, life enhancing, or transformative about this event or experience? Collect stories such as these to create environments where successful conditions for learning can be replicated.

Assumption #6: Adult learners are self-directing.

This assumption is the life force of andragogy, the heart and soul of lifelong learning, and therefore the spirit of leading. Literacy leaders need to understand that the essence of adult education is adults having input in their learning and choosing their own course or learning process based on personal/situational needs and desires. This understanding puts all else into perspective for literacy leaders. Adults need to be in charge of their own learning.

This principle allows us to consider power and positioning. It is the adult learner who is in charge, in power. As the adult learner creates his or her own learning trajectory, the literacy leader runs alongside ready and willing to share information and resources, ready to model reading, writing, or classroom management strategies by organizing activities to meet the learner's requests and desires. This requires the literacy leader to dismiss the idea that he or she is "the sage on the stage" and instead envision working alongside a colleague or student as facilitator, coach, and guide.

As teachers are in charge of their own learning, how can the literacy leader honor this while following directives from administrators? There are several options.

As one option, before initiating a change, literacy leaders can request to have conversations with administrators to discuss teacher empowerment and the benefit of shared leadership and decision making. Literacy leaders should share the principles of andragogy with all stakeholders so everyone works from a knowledge base regarding how adults learn best.

In understanding the principles of adult learning, administrators might be more inclined to value and therefore fund professional development that honors adult learners even if it's more expensive to secure substitute teachers or purchase resources. The leader can help create an adult-learning think tank to brainstorm ways to pool resources within a building to maximize learning potential. This can be done through the creation of lab-site classrooms, nurturing teacher leaders, fostering professional development at faculty meetings, engaging administrators in learning literacy content, and, of course, celebrating success. While it is best to have the support of administrators, leaders should remember that even if they don't, they can still position themselves to keep andragogy and the celebration going.

Another option might be that the literacy leader can help teachers and administrators recognize what they already know about a given literacy topic, and then identify learning trajectories through conversations, classroom visits, and survey-based assessments. Once teachers and administrators have an idea of what they want and need, then the literacy leader can offer a variety of professional development activities from which they can self-select to get to the end goal of learning a new practice. The leader should offer individual teachers two or three options, or perhaps a menu of learning-process choices, leaving the teacher to choose and thus self-direct his or her own learning. For example, Case Scenario D shows how the literacy leader offered Trish several options to learn more about effective minilessons, then left it up to Trish to choose her own learning path.

Finally, leaders should remember that change is a process requiring time, energy, patience, and human resources. Teachers and administrators will vary in their motivation and desire to learn situation by situation. The key to keeping adults on a self-directed path lies in the creation of a total school culture that embraces lifelong learning, with the start of this culture being just one teacher's move toward self-directed learning. Change occurs even when we nurture one teacher at a time.

The Artist as Specialist

Literacy leaders—the artists who are responsible and/or take it upon themselves to paint the vision of the literacy-learning community—must be adult learning specialists. To design and implement high-quality learning activities for job-embedded professional development, the literacy leader needs to know that adults learn best when literacy leaders

1. provide clear rationale as to why they are learning about a particular topic or new practice, weaving rationale throughout all professional learning activities before the learning begins;

2. honor the background knowledge and wealth of experience adult learners carry with them to each professional development activity;

3. respect the unique patterns or timing of participants' own readiness and recognition of readiness to learn;

4. build healthy relationships with all members of the faculty, as leading work truly begins before adult learners experience a need for change (a relationship needs to be in place for the work to move forward at a moment's notice);

5. encourage adult learners by gently tapping into their internal needs; and

6. roll out professional development experiences so adult learners can be self-directing at all times.

Closing Thoughts

Monet's quote at the beginning of this chapter helped us reflect on how adult learners come together to form a complete picture of a literacy-learning community by offering their individual talents. Now that you understand how adults learn, you can apply this knowledge to create a culture of continuous improvement in your district.

Next, we invite you to hear the voices of literacy leaders in the field as you read and contemplate The Ethical Literacy Leader and Critical Voices features in this chapter. Following each feature are questions in the Cultivate Your Leadership Skills section to prompt your thinking as you work toward nurturing a mosaic of adult learners in your context. To read more about the contributors' backgrounds, see the About the Contributors section.

The Ethical Literacy Leader
How Do I Keep on Working?
—MARY ANN LUCIANO

Mary Ann is director of the Catskill Regional Teacher Center in Otsego County, New York. Her work as a literacy leader includes showcasing teachers who are literacy leaders.

How can teacher literacy leaders keep on working when the external framework in which they work bumps up against their ethics? As a director of a large consortium teacher center in New York State, my work for the past 20 years has been to nurture teachers and their professional learning. Teacher centers are "for teachers by teachers," with the work governed and directed for and by teachers.

Recently, in a research capacity, I have been reviewing New York State's four-year testing reports on schools. In many cases, the schools have been identified under No Child Left Behind as needing improvement in English language arts—they are "on the list" and range from elementary schools to high schools. What is now a surprise to me is that many schools are on the list this year because of a change in last year's test scoring. They are now deemed "in need of improvement" and differ from those schools that have been on the list year after year. This group of schools in need of improvement is where my teacher constituents work. They are poor, rural schools that struggle to meet their budget year after year and are the schools most impacted by the state aid formula. A large percentage of their budget relies on state aid because they are in poor communities that do not have the wealth to raise the needed revenue on their own. Last year, these districts made draconian cuts in teaching positions and the resources to support learning.

Will these teachers now be regarded as ineffective or developing because their test scores do not meet the new Common Core State Standards? Will they, because of continuing loss of resources, have to take on larger class sizes and not do their jobs as well, leading to a spiral of students not meeting the test score benchmarks? How do I keep on working, knowing that the very teacher-evaluation systems adopted—that teacher centers must support because we receive our funding from the state—will work against the teacher center ethics of care and nurturing and have more to do with the test scores and less to do with working for better teaching? Should I keep on working in such a system? What is my responsibility in helping to change what is evident?

I believe I have to continue; to continue to nurture and support teachers as much as I can while also showing where the system is making errors. My first step will be to show teachers how their students' test achievement patterns affect them. Second, I will need to work with the teachers on finding out what parts of the assessment their students are "not getting." Fortunately, with the new Common Core State Standards and common interim formative assessments, teachers have some guide posts to

provide answers on what is needed. Also, using response to intervention, a strategy for identifying students who have learning disability needs, the teachers and I together can problem-solve to find out what works best for individual students.

Every teacher needs an honest chance to learn and change. Test scores do not show all a teacher is capable of. I found an excellent chart for "Propositions that justify the use of measures for evaluating teacher effectiveness" by Laura Goe of the National Comprehensive Center for Teacher Quality. Goe (2011) proposes a system wherein all the pieces mesh together: learning standards that are well defined with student assessments that correctly manifest student learning and show development over time. If these measures are valid and reliable with precision and fairness, then they can be used to show a teacher's influence on student learning.

The standards and assessment measures must be aligned to accurately portray student growth that is attributable to the teachers. However, before the system is deemed as such, it must be proven reliable and valid. Do the state tests meet this standard of validity and reliability? If they do not, as a teacher literacy leader I must advocate and demand that they do, that they are fair and accurate not only for their attribution to teachers but what they mean for students who are graded by these test scores. This means moving out of my comfort zone and learning a lot more about testing.

It is also imperative that I help teachers. I must help teachers learn how to gather evidence of their teaching. I plan to accomplish this through portfolio-building sessions with teachers and by videotaping and critiquing teaching practices. Yes, I will keep on working to support the teachers and students in my consortium. Now, possibly more than ever, they need me to advocate for them.

Cultivate Your Leadership Skills

1. What type of teacher advocacy centers exist in your area? What roles do they play as literacy leaders in your community?

2. How does Mary Ann's perspective fit with the principles of adult learning presented in this chapter?
3. What are the multiple levels of literacy leadership that exist in Mary Ann's story?

Critical Voices

Maintaining Respectful Relationships—Or "You're Not the Boss of Me!"

—CAROLYN CHRYST

Carolyn supervises, coaches, and mentors adult learners in various education contexts. She is an assistant professor in the Division of Education at the State University of New York College at Oneonta.

In my diverse roles as a literacy leader over my career as an educator, I have learned how critically important it is to be acutely aware of and able to apply the principles of adult learning and group dynamics to mentorship and leadership situations. All literacy leaders who work with adult learners will be able to learn from my experience.

Recently, I received a scathing e-mail from an elementary teacher in whose classroom I had worked several times over the years as part of a university-school partnership. According to the e-mail, the teacher (let's call him Larry) was extremely upset with me from a previous encounter and was now declining to work with me again (let's call me Curly). Larry claimed I had mocked and disrespected a colleague and his school! I was shocked. How could he accuse me of this when I purposely always go out of my way to praise this school and its faculty any chance I get? I sincerely believe the work they are doing is extraordinary. What could account for such a discrepancy in perceptions?

There is a third teacher involved in this story (let's call him Moe). I had previously coached Moe on using an inquiry approach in his teaching. Moe had demonstrated very little respect for the inquiry approach, so you can imagine my glee when, one lovely morning, I stopped by Moe's classroom to say hello as I was on my way to work with another student in the building. My objective for just popping my head into Moe's room was to build trust and camaraderie. To my delight, I saw Moe participating in a lesson that was 100 percent inquiry. I was shocked, to tell the truth, and very excited. In the hall after his lesson, I said to Moe (with Larry nearby), "I love that lesson! Did you see how engaged the students were? You know you can find hundreds of lessons like that on YouTube." I puffed up with pride for Moe.

Apparently, Larry and Moe's interpretation of my comment about YouTube was on the opposite end of the spectrum from what I had intended. Moe felt I was belittling the lesson by comparing it to those found on YouTube. By extension, either Moe or Larry, or both, had interpreted my comment to mean I was belittling the school. My question is: Why hadn't Larry checked with me before he flew off the handle and sent the scathing e-mail? I thought we had built a trusting work relationship.

I've come to realize the tirade was a complex relationship much like the Three Stooges. A stooge is someone who follows a leader. As the university professor presumed leader/coach, I am an invited guest in the teachers' classrooms. The teachers are the actual leaders of the classroom environment. So how does a teacher negotiate whom to follow when he or she perceives a disconnect in direction and application of theory? When teachers forge a tight bond, the potential of a "them-against-us" (i.e., university/theory/elitism versus real-world/practical/in-the-trenches) attitude is very high. I had clearly not understood the perceived power structure or Larry and Moe's need to defy it. I always think of university partners as my peers and colleagues.

Of course, this awkward confusion has been cleared up. We all honestly voiced our intentions and perceptions, and now I am again working with these teachers. However, I've learned from this experience. I have come to be very aware, respectful, and cautious of the social dynamics and perceived lines of authority and power of the university-school partnership. I know now that trying to serve two masters can make stooges of us all!

Cultivate Your Leadership Skills

1. What factors are involved in the "power structure" and "differential of power" that existed among Larry, Moe, and Curly?
2. How might Carolyn's experience relate to a K–12 literacy-leadership community?
3. How do the six assumptions presented in this chapter relate to Carolyn's experience?
4. Carolyn says "trying to serve two masters can make stooges of us all." What do you think she means by this statement? How can this paradigm be prevented and avoided in literacy-leadership communities?

Questions for Reflection and Discussion

1. Which principles of adult education seem easy to embrace as part of your philosophy as a literacy leader? Which principles may be more difficult to embrace? Why?

2. When literacy leaders embrace this philosophy, what difficulties might they anticipate arising in relation to each of the six principles?

3. When asked by a principal to introduce yourself and share your literacy-leadership philosophy, what might you say?

4. Read Case Scenario E that follows. What would be the most ethical way for James to approach this issue?

Case Scenario E

James is a middle school literacy leader. He has been in the same district across six schools for three years. James is responsible for collaboratively planning literacy initiatives with the elementary and high school literacy supervisors and leaders across the district per mandates from the superintendent and principals.

James attended an out-of-district workshop where he learned the six key understandings of adult education and how to use these principles to create cycles of professional development for teachers with whom he works. Throughout the workshop,

James was asked to reflect upon his own identity, beliefs, values, and leading philosophy. Initially, he was not happy with what he realized about his leading philosophy and work. He realized his methods were mostly "one-size-fits-all" in nature.

James now views district-wide, top-down initiatives, with little to no teacher input, as oppressive and ineffective. He would like to make a change. James works to set up professional development with others who continue to use a "one-size-fits-all" approach to professional development. He would like to shift professional development across the district to a paradigm that honors adult learners.

5. Coming full circle, reread Monet's quote with which the chapter begins. Now that you've read and reflected on this chapter, in what ways do you see the mosaic of adult learners in your school or context woven into a "matter of habit," or their potential to be?

Practical Applications

How might this chapter apply to your teaching context and experience? Try these activities: and success with your larger professional learning community.

Classroom Activity

Take a moment to reread the six principles of adult learning. Which principles resonate with you as an adult learner? Use the six principles to design an action research project within the context of your classroom. What topic do you feel ready to explore? List three steps you will take to learn more about this topic. List three steps you will take to integrate this topic into your teaching. List three reflection and assessment strategies you will use to evaluate your action research project. Celebrate your findings

Professional Development Activity

How wonderful it would be to openly discuss the six principles of andragogy within the context of a faculty meeting or other staff development experience! Create an active, lively introduction to these six principles and cultivate conversation to identity ways in which the key principles resonate, or do not resonate, with faculty. An active, lively presentation may include PowerPoint, role play, sharing stories, charting ideas, and brainstorming ways to apply the six principles of andragogy to ongoing professional learning in your local school context.

References

Barth, Roland, S. (1990). *Improving schools from within: Teachers, parents, and principals can make the difference.* San Francisco, CA: Jossey-Bass Publishers.

Goe, L. (2011, April 21). *Evaluating teacher/leader's effectiveness.* Webinar for Washington Teacher-Principal Evaluation Project. Nashville, TN: National Comprehensive Center for Teacher Quality. Retrieved from http://www.tqsource.org/presentationsFromField/pdfs/PresentationToWashingtonTeacher-Principal-EvaluationProject_April_21_2011.pdf

Knowles, M., Holton, E., & Swanson, R. A. (2011). *The adult learner: The definitive classic in adult education and human resource development.* Burlington, MA: Elsevier.

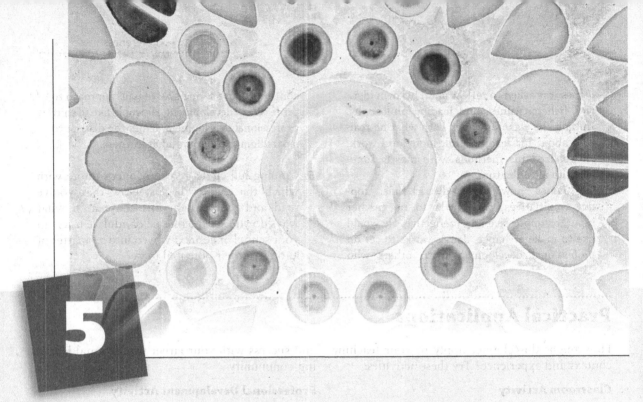

5

Sketching Critical and Collaborative Communication

66 *The tongue can paint what the eye can't see.* 99

—CHINESE PROVERB

Introduction

How does the opening Chinese proverb connect with this chapter on critical and collaborative communication in literacy leadership? Your response might be totally different from your colleagues' and the authors' responses. That's the thing about communication: It can be nebulous. Two people reading or hearing the same words can hear, understand, or interpret them in totally different ways. The point the proverb makes, however, might be interpreted as this: One's words can have a powerful impact because they can reveal things of which another might not have previously been aware. In light of this, we must be mindful of our words.

Through their critical and collaborative communication skills and their passion for literacy and teaching, literacy leaders can bring people and resources together to paint visions and experiences. This chapter will heighten your awareness of and sharpen your communication skills within the context of literacy-learning communities.

Artful Communication

As a literacy leader, it is essential to have effective communication skills. Communicating with others is a major part of our job. We listen, provide feedback, teach, model, discuss, persuade, encourage, create written documents, and present information. We may find, however, that we are infrequently trained or provided support to learn how to communicate effectively with colleagues and administrators.

In many cases literacy leaders are expected to be able to design and implement change in school literacy programs at the classroom or district level. We may become the middle person in charge of these changes, expected to orchestrate discussions and present information. We may have to know how to be able to communicate with others in ways that will influence and guide them to develop and commit to goals that typically reflect a need for flexibility. If we're lucky, a few will embrace the changes or new ideas. More than likely, however, most may be uncertain; and some may be resistant. How do we communicate and foster communication among colleagues that will bring everyone together to work toward common goals?

Communication happens when ideas are exchanged through mutually understood language, symbols (i.e., in writing), or behaviors. As you read this paragraph, for example, the authors are communicating ideas to you through symbols. If you talk with others about what you've read, you are communicating your ideas to them through language and possibly behaviors. Communication basically involves a back-and-forth transfer of messages that both or all parties understand

and can build upon. We like Brookfield and Preskill's (2005) idea about promoting discussion groups for democratic learning. We encourage the creation of conversation circles to just come together to talk with no set agenda. People bring different topics they deem important to just discuss to share ideas or gain insight. This circle work tends to open up deep learning as discussion digs for insight and solutions to solve problems, think about issues, and move forward.

As literacy leaders, we must do more than transfer information or encourage colleagues to just exchange ideas. Sharing is helpful as we become resources for each other, but just giving someone a recipe doesn't mean they'll be able to create the same entrée. Also, it doesn't mean that even if you get the recipe right your family will like the entrée. The point is that a literacy method that works in one classroom context may not be appropriate in another classroom. The teacher's mode of presentation may affect the outcomes, or the method might not be effective with this particular group of students.

Therefore, the type of communication vital to effective literacy leaders encourages self-awareness and the sharing of information and ideas as a base to building upon each other's experiences and knowledge to meet the needs of our students. As Judy Moeller, a coach from Watertown, Connecticut, told us,

> literacy leaders do need a wide repertoire of strategies and skills to build trusting relationships. We need to be viewed by the teachers as a supportive resource and not the person who will be formally supervising them with teacher observations.

Judy forms trusting relationships via communication strategies. She listed the following practices as examples:

- Listening actively while the teacher is reviewing the concern or question with you
- Repeating or summarizing what is talked about with the teacher so you speak the same language and arrive at the same understanding of the communication event
- Laughing with them, commiserating with them, and cheering them on
- Asking for their feedback during and after a lesson you modeled
- Collaborating and planning the lessons together
- Providing honest, constructive feedback

Finally, along this same vein, we encourage you to read what Margaret Wheatley (2002) has to say about building relationships with people. She states that openheartedness solves problems when we genuinely care for other human beings. We do not exist in isolation and, therefore, innately want to be together. Hope comes from truthfulness; connecting with others gives us joy. She says that we need to slow down to take time to know each other because the fast pace of modern life is causing us to lose the time to think and learn. Consider what all this means in the context of schools and education. We often complain about there not being enough time. We rush from one meeting to another without stopping to ask each other, "How are you doing today, friend?" and waiting for a sincere reply. As you move through this chapter, keep Wheatley's thoughts in mind. Think about the ways you, as a literacy leader, can build meaningful relationships with your colleagues as you work together to improve students' literacy skills and development.

Etching Proactive Communication

Based on our own experiences and what we have learned from literacy leaders across the nation, the type of proactive leadership we are promoting in this book involves communication

- that is motivating, supportive, honest, and cooperative;
- that encourages reflection;
- that opens conversations up so multiple perspectives can be considered;
- that encourages everyone to inquire about literacy learning by seriously questioning and discussing possibilities and options; and
- that creates a forum for colleagues to come to a consensus about what is best for the students.

We refer to this type of communication as being critical and collaborative. It is critical in that it is analytic, evaluative, and encourages questioning. It is collaborative in that it leads to the intersection of common goals through productive partnerships. Read this chapter's The Common Core State Standards Connection that discusses the topic of communication as it relates to the standards.

. By promoting critical and collaborative communication, literacy leaders provide opportunities for educators to develop authoritative confidence and rich understandings that can be applied to their teaching. For communication to be highly effective in a context in which a literacy leader is working with teachers, several components must be in place. To begin, obviously, there needs to be a transmitter or speaker (sometimes a writer) who has a message to share; a recipient who will receive the message; and, of course, a message. In a literacy context, the message might be a teacher's concern, a literacy leader's observation, or an administrator's question. We will use the terms "speaker," "receiver," and "message" throughout this chapter to keep roles clear.

Critical Communication

Proactive communication that occurs as a way to anticipate and alleviate problems or crises is critical. Once conversation has begun and the speaker and receiver are

The Common Core State Standards Connection

In All Thy Getting . . . Get an Understanding

—TRACEY JOHNSON

Tracey's career in education spans over 22 years. She has taught at all educational levels, developed curriculum, provided professional development to persistently low-achieving schools, and mentored teachers. Tracey is currently employed at the New York State Education Department.

As literacy leaders, we have a responsibility to get an understanding of those whom we teach. It is incumbent upon us to listen and observe. The art of communicating effectively requires an understanding of the interrelationship between listening and speaking. Linguists categorize this distinction as "receptive language" and "expressive language." Receptive language is language that is heard, processed, and understood by an individual; expressive language is language that is generated and produced by an individual.

The Common Core State Standards contain six anchor standards for speaking and listening. They are divided into two groups: comprehension and collaboration, and presentation of knowledge and ideas. In the

first group, students are expected to talk together to understand texts. In the latter group, students are expected to make oral presentations using digital media and visual displays.

Teachers will need to make strategic instructional decisions about how they are going to plan for rigorous, curricular-aligned conversations that will gradually evolve from partnership discussions to larger group discussions where students can independently build on each other's ideas and express their own ideas clearly and persuasively. As students are exposed to explicit instruction in conversation, the teacher's role becomes more of a facilitator and not a leader of discussions and conversations (Calkins, Ehrenworth, & Lehman, 2012).

listening and providing feedback to each other, the parties take time to assess and evaluate the messages being communicated back and forth. Critical communication falls into the evaluating category of Bloom's (Anderson & Krathwohl, 2001; Bloom & Krathwohl, 1956) cognitive domain, in which learners make judgments about the value of ideas based on certain standards by appraising, justifying, comparing, and contrasting them with others. Critical communication may involve parties asking themselves and each other questions such as

Teacher: How does this pertain to my classroom? What new skills will I need to acquire to be able to integrate this new method? How will this new approach affect student learning compared to what I was doing? Is learning this new method worth my effort?

Literacy Leader:	What are my beliefs about this new approach? How do I balance my personal and professional relationships with my colleagues? How do I provide honest feedback without offending teachers?
Administrator:	How can the district provide effective professional development for our teachers based on the suggested changes? Will our school culture encourage or hinder participation in this new initiative? How can we promote open-mindedness among our staff and build a literacy-learning community that supports all?

Each of these concerns requires evaluation and critical communication. Teachers, literacy leaders, and administrators appraise the values of themselves, their colleagues, and their community to justify the most effective solution or path. Dialogs take place that lead to the answers to these questions. The goal of this dialog is to bring out everyone's ideas, concerns, and feelings; lay them on the table; look at them through a high-power lens; and come to a meeting of the minds or, perhaps, a compromise. Drawing out others' perspectives and building agreement or consensus leads to improved ideas, shared ownership, and commitment among all parties. Critical communication might look like the following dialog between a teacher and a literacy leader:

Teacher 1:	I really like what I'm doing now with my students. I find it hard to justify changing my writing program to a workshop approach when I have so much time invested in developing the program I use now.
Literacy Leader:	You have put a lot of time and energy into your writing program. Specifically, what do you like about what you are doing now?
Teacher:	Students have choices about what they write. They really like that.
Literacy Leader:	Choice is important. Writing workshop provides choice, too. What else do you like about what you're doing?
Teacher:	I observe students' needs through their writing and teach strategies and skills based on their needs.
Literacy Leader:	Writing workshop minilessons come from students' writing needs, but instead of teaching skills to the whole class, you can differentiate instruction through small-group instruction. Let me explain . . .

Later . . .

Literacy Leader:	How does what I've shown you compare with what you are doing already?

> Teacher: I like the ideas of small-group minilessons and peer conferences. But I'm still unsure about how to manage a workshop approach. It seems so unstructured.

Notice how the literacy leader recognizes what the teacher values about her writing program, offers opportunities to compare and contrast the teacher's program with the writing workshop approach, and then leads the conversation toward a discussion of the value of writing workshop, inviting the teacher to critique and evaluate each approach. The literacy leader's approach helps the teacher reflect on her practice and analyze what she is doing without diminishing what the teacher values. This opens the conversation up and causes both parties to look critically at best methods. The teacher seems willing to hear more about writing workshop.

Collaborative Communication

Proactive communication is collaborative, strengthened by the voices and ideas of many. Collaborative communication falls within creating, the highest category of Bloom's new taxonomy of cognitive domain as revised by Anderson and Krathwohl (2001; Bloom & Krathwohl, 1956). Through collaborative communication, colleagues reorganize and synthesize ideas as they generate, plan, produce, and move forward. Collaborative communication may involve parties asking themselves and each other questions such as the following:

> Teacher: How can we make the best use of the time we spend reading to our students? What do others do to integrate literacy in math? Who would be the best person to work with to learn about teaching reading comprehension? Will he or she let me observe some lessons?

> Literacy Leader: Would you be willing to share the ways you integrate literacy in your content area with others? We've been working on ways to teach reading comprehension. What strategies do you see as being most effective with your students?

> Administrator: How are the students progressing in reading fluency across grade levels? What evidence do we have that they are making progress? What steps do we still need to take?

Collaborative communication might look like the following dialog among two teachers and their school's literacy coach:

> Teacher 1:   I was reading an article about using critical literacy in a first-grade classroom. Do you think children at that age are too young to discuss issues like homelessness?

Teacher 2:   I'm not sure I'd be comfortable answering controversial questions.

Literacy Coach: What would be our goals for incorporating critical literacy in first grade? Let's start by looking at the Common Core State Standards.

Notice how the first teacher raises a question and asks her colleagues' opinion. The coach brings the conversation to a higher level by suggesting it is a matter of setting goals for critical thinking. This leads the teachers to begin to plan a course of action for creating a list of topics and scaffolding critical thinking across the grade levels. Through collaborative conversation they move toward creating and producing.

Now that we have a clear understanding of what critical and collaborative communication are and what they might look like in a coaching experience, let's take a look at specific ideas for developing our skills as communicators.

Etching the Communication Process

The Speaker's Message

As George Bernard Shaw (n.d.) once said, "The problem with communication . . . is the *illusion* that it has been accomplished." How do we know if what we mean to communicate, or our intended message, is what actually gets transmitted? Perhaps we aren't clearly stating what we mean to say or write. Also, we cannot just assume that the receiver interprets the intended meaning from our message. Red Auerbach, one of the National Basketball Association's Ten Greatest Leaders in History, once said, "It's not what you tell them . . . it's what they hear" (n.d.). That seems to say it all: our intended messages are sometimes misinterpreted or *mis*-heard. Based on the world view we hold, we quickly latch onto information that fits perfectly within our current world view while easily dismissing what does not fit.

Has this ever happened to you? Have you ever been in a situation in which you totally misinterpreted what someone said to you? This can happen for a number of reasons. For example, it could be that you took the person's words for face value and didn't take the total context of the situation into consideration. Maybe the person was just joking but you took him or her seriously. Or, maybe you misunderstood because you weren't aware of some background information or you weren't familiar with some of the concepts or vocabulary used. It happens.

Literacy leaders should be acutely aware of the context of the situation. First of all, think through your message and consider what issues and anxieties the receivers may be feeling. Know your receivers. Are you threatening them or their beliefs? Do you anticipate any resistance or hostility will come from your message? Often a literacy leader's job involves going into a teacher's classroom and demonstrating a literacy lesson with his or her students. Consider how this might be interpreted by a teacher. While we hope the teacher looks at the demonstration as an opportunity to learn new skills and strategies, inevitably some teachers might feel vulnerable and look at it as a threat. Anticipating these issues and feelings will help you remain focused if they do arise during your meetings with teachers.

Second, be aware of your feelings. As a literacy leader, be prepared to answer or help facilitate discussion of an onslaught of questions. You may feel nervous or even defensive, especially if you are new at coaching, are unsure of the best route to take, or are instituting a new directive that you don't totally buy into. It helps if you can look at questioners as simply people wanting more information, even if they appear to ask for it in challenging or abrupt ways (Hamlin, 2006). And, in your responses, use words that are democratically charged rather than those that are charged by the power of being a leader. When you begin to feel threatened or nervous, try responding with comments such as the following:

- I hear your concern. Let's see what ideas others can offer.

   OR

   I'll see what I can find out and get back to you. (Use when you don't have information or the answer right at your fingertips.)

- Maybe others can share what they have done and then we can talk about how their ideas would fit your situation. (Give specific examples; that shows we're all in the same boat and others are trying new things, too.)

- Let's seek clarification and open a dialog with administration. (Use when you ethically don't feel comfortable answering a question, especially about policy or protocol.)

- As we all want what's best for our students, let's . . . (Use when the conversation needs refocusing toward positive outcomes.)

Next, choose your words wisely. Being coached can be intimidating for some teachers. Some may be very sensitive to the fact that you are in the picture to introduce change and new skills to be learned. Be sure to thank the teacher for being willing to talk with you and being open to reflecting on his or her practice with you. Focus on the fact that you are both there for the benefit of the students. You have a common goal: to improve students' literacy and learning. Be genuinely gracious and complimentary. Use phrases such as these:

Thank you for your hospitality.

I'm eager to learn from you.

Be passionate and show your excitement about learning and trying something new:

> Enthusiasm can be infectious, you know.
>
> This lesson is going to be really exciting. We're going to learn so much by seeing how this works with your class.

Use "we" instead of "I" whenever possible. This simple use of a plural pronoun implies to the teacher that you are on his or her side, and this is a team effort. You aren't telling your colleague what to do; you're both learning together. Also, avoid the use of the word "but" in situations where you want to insert a new idea, as in "That's good to do, *but . . .*"

Instead, consider what you can say or ask that will lead the teacher and help him or her view things in a new way without arming or alarming him or her. Often our words set up an "us-versus-them" distinction that's not even conscious. Little words can make a big difference in how our words are received and interpreted by others (Johnston, 2004).

Finally, after the meeting or conversation, take time to reflect about the process and the outcomes. Specifically, ask yourself these questions:

> Did the meeting go as I had planned?
>
> Did I get my messages across? What did I do well?
>
> How do I know I got my messages across?
>
> What could I have done better? How will I improve my communication next time?
>
> What might be blocking more effective communication?
>
> What do I still need to learn how to do?
>
> How can I learn more on this topic?

Build a reflection structure into your regular routine. You might network with a colleague from another district; or, if you choose to reflect more privately, we suggest you begin a literacy leader's journal. Write in it regularly to analyze your communication experiences and reflect on the progress you and your district are making; your professional and leadership goals; and your deep-down secret hopes, fears, and confessions around coaching. Journals are helpful to "hold thinking still" so that you can be introspective about what is really happening (Clark & Ivanic, 1997). But journals are less useful if we don't take some action based on our reflective process. Reread pieces of your journal several times a year and note the journey you've been on. Are your communication skills improving? Make plans for change, or it probably won't happen. A journal can help you recognize if and when change is needed, but only you can act upon it.

Figure 5.1 highlights some more specific tips for transmitting messages.

FIGURE 5.1 **Tips for Transmitting Messages Effectively**

Check your body language.

- Maintain eye contact.
- Keep smiling.
- Assume a poised but comfortable position.
- Are you a head-nodder? Sometimes we nod while we listen because we are listening, but it may show agreement when we are not meaning to agree. Remain neutral when the situation calls for it.
- Try mirroring the receiver's body language if he or she looks relaxed and confident.

Make your messages visual.

- Provide diagrams, handouts, or other tangible resources.
- Begin more formal meetings with a written agenda to clarify goals.
- Follow up your meeting by distributing written notes highlighting meeting outcomes.
- Provide chart paper, markers, and other tools for receivers to use during the meeting. Check interpretations of the messages as they are recorded.

Build trust by admitting when you don't have an answer or solution. Build confidence by following up with resources.

Be yourself. Don't assume a false personna. Don't compete.

Encourage others to ask questions when you are being unclear. Remind them that there is no such thing as a stupid question.

The Listener and the Response

We usually listen on automatic pilot, meaning we don't think much about it. In a professional learning situation, though, the literacy leader listens manually in a hands-on-the-wheel way. Teachers will respond to literacy leaders who listen to them. Everyone wants to know they have been heard. To meet the needs of our students, colleagues, and administrators, we have to be sure we understand what is being communicated. Also, we must practice professional, competent ways to respond to messages we receive. Here are some suggestions and examples of how to listen responsively:

Listen to and for Ideas, Perspectives, and Insights.   Mind what the speaker is saying. During a conversation, literacy leaders might hear teachers voice many negative or resistant statements, such as "I've tried that before, and it doesn't work. They can't work in groups." The trick is to listen to the messages behind the words. Do they really mean this? "How do I manage the rest of the class while I'm running guided reading groups?" Or: "When I tried that before, I didn't understand how to . . ." As a teacher is talking, try to see beyond his or her words to find

FIGURE 5.2   Tips for Being an Active, Hands-on Listener

Always maintain eye contact and smile.

Take notes only if necessary. Try to write between expressions.

Don't interrupt the speaker unless you have to ask a clarifying question.

Be sure to listen first and evaluate later.

When the speaker is done, paraphrase what you think was said.

Focus on what the speaker is saying, rather than what your response will be.

Lean toward the speaker slightly.

out what the underlying message is. Are the words reflecting doubt or resistance? Visualize yourself turning off the automatic pilot and grabbing the wheel. Listen critically. Also, consider how having an agenda of what you want to say interferes with listening deeply. How do we navigate that situation? In our experience, it is extremely difficult to be thinking about what you want to say or accomplish and at the same time be listening deeply. It can be difficult to be open to real dialog. Figure 5.2 highlights tips for active, hands-on listening.

Check the Speaker's Intent.   Question the speaker's intended message. However, never assume your interpretation of the underlying message is accurate. Misunderstandings may occur if you fail to check the differences between what you hear and what the speaker intended. How do you check?

1. Paraphrase or restate the message and follow it with a clarifying question, such as, "So, you've tried group work before and it wasn't successful. Can you describe what happened?"
2. Watch for slips of the tongue, erratic gestures, changes in voice, and fleeting facial expressions in the listener's response to your message (Ekman, 2000). These may be clues that you have misinterpreted the message and are leading the conversation astray.

We also noted that critical communication helps a teacher become aware of his or her feelings and perspectives. When responding to the speaker, encourage him or her to be introspective and mine out those personal and professional aspects that shape the teacher's pedagogy. Ask the teacher: "What are your beliefs about how children learn to read? What is your favorite part of teaching writing? Why?"

Respond to Questions Responsibly.   Be sure to listen to the whole question. Take in the entire question before you begin to think about your answer. Also, notice how the question is asked. Is the speaker hostile or insecure? It is good practice to pause and clarify the question, perhaps restating it. Sometimes questions can ramble, and it's difficult to know exactly what the person really wants to know. Assume the responsibility for clarification on yourself by saying: "That's a really good question. There's a lot to it. Let me make sure I got it right. You're asking . . ."

Etching Literacy Contexts

Now that we're all clear about how to communicate critically and collaboratively and what we want to achieve through our communication, let's look at a number of contexts in which literacy leaders practice communicating with colleagues and administrators. Each context will require us to tweak our communication skills ever so slightly to meet the needs of the situation.

Large-Group Discussions

As literacy leaders, sometimes we work with large groups of people. Some districts hold workshops on conference days and bring certain groups together for professional development in a particular area. The literacy leader is sometimes responsible for facilitating such meetings. Here are some ideas for communicating with a large group.

- Over-prepare. Have written notes that outline key points. Anticipate questions that might arise. Bring enough resources and handouts with you for everyone.
- Take the role of a facilitator as much as possible. Most adults don't want to be lectured to. Engage the group with small-group discussions. Allow others to play the expert and share their experiences and knowledge.
- Set a purpose for the meeting. "We're here today to . . . because. . . ."
- Provide a risk-free environment so everyone's ideas are heard and considered.
- Bring closure to the meeting by summarizing progress and plans for action.
- Provide many examples.
- Be passionate but genuine.
- Know your group and what individuals have to offer in the conversation. Approaching and asking colleagues ahead of time if they would be willing to share a certain experience with the group gives them time to prepare, builds

their confidence, and provides opportunities to practice and model collaborative communication.

- Encourage questioning. Encourage the sharing of multiple perspectives and options. The best ideas come from thinking outside of the box.
- Effectively balance the dialogue and communication with the hands-on work or tasks that might need to be accomplished.
- Follow up the meeting by distributing notes from the meeting and plans for action.

Working with Small Groups or Individuals

Literacy leaders often work with grade-level teams of teachers or individual teachers to plan lessons and curriculum that integrate literacy instruction and best practices. The coach may participate in grade-level meetings or observe, coteach, or model lessons and strategies. These types of meetings and lessons should be well planned beforehand, then discussed thoroughly after they occur. Plan for critical and collaborative communication:

- Write out plans and document notes from all meetings. Ask someone to be in charge of keeping minutes at each meeting. E-mail or otherwise distribute minutes to all parties and keep a master file yourself.
- Arrange for a time to debrief after a lesson has been observed, cotaught, or modeled. During the debriefing, provide words of support and motivation to keep the conversations and attempts at a new practice going without deflating the teachers or causing them to feel intimidated to take risks in front of the coach or at all. Create a systematic feedback loop that works in your situation. Always be sure to ask the teacher, "What do you think went well?" Then give praise with what we call "lean feedback." In other words, don't lay the feedback on like thick peanut butter. Just spread a light layer of jelly.

Don't say: "You're going to have to really change the way you teach spelling. First of all, giving 25 words a week to second graders is just way too much. And asking them to use all the words in a sentence is useless."

Instead, say: "I like that you spend so much time focusing on spelling instruction. Are you finding the students use the words from the spelling list in their writing? When you said, 'Spelling always counts,' it showed the students you value accurate spelling in whatever they write, and they should, too. How could we get them to improve their spelling in their weekly writing through direct spelling instruction? I wonder if we could . . ."

By beginning with praise, you validate what the teacher is already doing. You show that you recognize that he or she is focusing on improving literacy, even if it is in a small way. Sandwich your message with praise and lean feedback to effectively communicate your insight. Couple the communication with collaborative phrases, such as "let's try" and "knowing your students, how would it work if . . ."

Dealing with Confrontation and Negotiation

Those of us who are passionate about literacy tend to have strong emotions about how it should be taught and what is best for our students. These passions sometimes ignite, causing conflicts and debates. While critical communication is valuable, when it reaches the point of nonproductive confrontation, nothing is gained. Therefore, we recommend literacy leaders should do the following:

■ Encourage civil discussion of hot topics. Preset the discussion with the idea that we are all professionals with the same goal in mind: helping the students.

■ Learn how to put yourself in the teacher's or administrator's place. See things from his or her point of view. What do you think is causing him or her to be resistant or argumentative? Discuss issues as appropriate. Dissect them so negotiation can begin.

■ Avoid debates. Speak thoughtfully, sensitively, and knowledgably. Don't get drawn into debating in front of others or being tempted to save face by sticking to your perspective. Calmly say, "Let's talk about this later when we have more time to figure this out together." Or: "That's a really complex point. We need more think time on that."

■ Bring evidence-based research to the table to support best practices when negotiating programs and practices.

Communicating Through Writing

We have integrated many ideas for communicating through writing in this chapter. However, we would just like to reiterate that documenting progress is very important. Be sure to keep meeting agendas, minutes, and other notes well organized and clearly labeled. You never know when you will be asked to backtrack or provide information to the school board or for colleagues' use. Written records also become a tool for reflecting on a district's progress. Keeping a history of events and decisions may prevent you from repeating mistakes and may guide you toward the best path. (Read Dawn Hamlin's Response to Intervention [RTI] and the Literacy Leader feature in this chapter on this topic.) Finally, sharing written documents from meetings can help clarify messages that might have been missed

Response to Intervention (RTI) and the Literacy Leader

Decision Making and Reviewing

—DAWN HAMLIN

Dawn is currently assistant professor at SUNY College at Oneonta. She is a former special education teacher who taught in both traditional public schools and residential facilities.

In RTI, if we have captured accurate, reliable, and valid data—*the student is always right.* Period. This can be hard for RTI team members to get used to, especially if they have not been trained to think in this clinical way. To some it seems very detached. However, in reality, focusing on objective rather than subjective measures will help us in more accurately discussing and determining effective evidence-based practice interventions.

Often, I will encounter teachers who will tell me that little Katie is doing "just fine" with reading. Yet, when we look at the data picture, we see a picture of a student who may be a very fluent reader and can answer literal comprehension questions like a pro, yet has trouble with predictions or inferential comprehension.

The dilemma is this: How can literacy leaders take these data pictures and have quality discussions about what to do next? This is not a blame game if the student has failed to respond to a particular intervention, but rather a mystery. How do we find the gaps in knowledge and then fill in the gaps using targeted evidence-based interventions? After the intervention phase (usually a few weeks to a marking period) has been completed, a data review should be conducted.

Key questions that should be discussed among the RTI team include the following:

1. Is the student making adequate progress? How can we accelerate progress to help students? What data have we referenced for typical weekly growth? (Hasbrouck and Tindal have a wonderful chart for oral-reading fluency measures available at http://www.jhasbrouck.com/ORF2005_dataBRT.pdf.)
2. What areas has the student had success with? Can we change the goal standard or should we look at a new, unrelated goal?
3. If the student has not been successful in meeting goals, can we safely say we followed the intervention procedures with high treatment fidelity? Or, should the team go back and try again?
4. What are our options for meeting the set goals? Can we add additional instructional time in the student's day that focuses on the critical skill? Is it time to add targeted instruction on a related skill that is a prerequisite for future skills?

or misunderstood and can update colleagues who had to be absent from meetings. In general, written communication can be easily misconstrued. Choose your wording wisely to craft your message, and reread what you write while thinking about how various readers might interpret what you've said.

Closing Thoughts

The Chinese proverb that begins this chapter refers to communication that is powerful. This phenomenon is the epitome of the nature of written communication. Therefore, we caution you to be aware that what you write today will be available for others to read and reread tomorrow, next week, next month, and next year. Written communication can be both a blessing and a curse: Things we write can support us and haunt us. Be cautious of the words you put into print. Read Janet Richards's The Ethical Literacy Leader in this chapter for examples of ethical communication through e-mailing. This unique feature not only shares Janet's experiences but briefly summarizes new knowledge about crafting ethical communication.

Next, we invite you to hear the voices of literacy leaders in the field as you read and contemplate The Ethical Literacy Leader and Critical Voices features in this chapter. Following each feature are questions in the Cultivate Your Leadership Skills section to prompt your thinking as you work toward sketching critical and collaborative communication in your context. To read more about the contributors' backgrounds, see the About the Contributors section.

The Ethical Literacy Leader
Crafting Ethical Communication
—JANET RICHARDS

Janet, professor of literacy and research at the University of South Florida, supervises field-based courses at a local community center where she mentors her graduate students in a Community of Practice model. In this caring structure, doctoral and master's students learn to become literacy leaders.

Ethics and literacy leadership are currently on the front burner of education. For example, the National Reading Conference sponsors a Special Interest Group devoted specifically to ethical issues related to literacy teaching and learning. One ongoing topic discussed by members of the group entails literacy leaders' ethical communication. Given the centrality of communicative expertise to teaching and learning, effective and ethical communication is particularly significant for literacy leaders. Ethical communication is a caring, other-oriented, nonjudgmental mode of interaction that communication experts term "interpersonal communication" (Beebe, Beebe, & Redmond, 2005). Interpersonal communication occurs when individuals engage in dialogue that is "based upon equality rather than superiority" (p. 7).

Yet, as technology increasingly moves forward, and ease and swiftness of communication become the norm, ethical communication may actually become impersonal and lack an ethos of relational care. Electronic messages are fraught with challenges because lack of nonverbal cues may cause misunderstanding. Communications disconnected from a communicator's actions, voice tone, posture, and gestures are often misconstrued (Richards, Bennett, & Shea, 2007; also see Silverman, 2000). Even more serious is that literacy leaders need to recognize the ease and swiftness of communication through the use of ipads, iphones, e-mail, blogs, Facebook, and the like that may become problematic when they do not carefully consider their communication style and the ethical consequences of their words.

Here are a few messages literacy leaders recently e-mailed teachers in a recent study I conducted that highlighted impersonal and interpersonal electronic communication. (All names in these messages are pseudonyms.)

Nancy, Next week what are your objectives? What will the students learn? Connie

Hi Lloyd. I need to have a conversation with you because you are having difficulties. Your problem is you interrupt your students when they answer your questions. Also, are you confused? Unprepared? Can you accept responsibilities? Janeal

You need to communicate more by e-mail, John. I need to tell you that you must communicate to me! You also need to learn reading comprehension strategies and how to be flexible. Dannequa

Joyce, Susan, and Kathy, This is all overwhelming helping you three as a literacy coach. This is not an easy job.

These four authentic examples of unethical, terse messages are in sharp contrast to the following interpersonal e-mail communication that promotes an interactive climate in which individuals feel safe, understood, and accepted.

Tyisha, May I offer some suggestions to you? Remember to start closing down the lesson at least 2 minutes before your reading lesson is over. You can have the kids help you pack

up. You are doing all of the chores yourself. Kids love to help and they need to learn to accept responsibility. Also, remember, you are doing a great job.

Hi Everyone, I am really proud of what we accomplished. When we started we were confused. I had no idea how to go about planning lessons with you, but now everything is falling into place. I am grateful to all of you. I gained a lot from observing you. Maurice

Mary, When we do things together—we do a great job teaching reading. Scott

Hey WOW Grace! You did a great job yesterday! I thought it was wonderful to observe you as you presented reading strategies. It was terrific. Can I help you in any way? We could try to meet if you can find the time. I appreciate all that you do. Thank you for working so hard. Gerald

The literacy leaders' messages show it is easy to distinguish the disparities between interpersonal, unethical messages and interpersonal, relational-caring ethical messages. Relational-caring ethical communication fosters a collaborative, interactive climate in which individuals feel safe, understood, and accepted (Richards et al., 2007; also see Beebe et al., 2005). It is not surprising, then, that interpersonal sensitivity and ethical communication skills are the foremost characteristics of exemplary literacy leaders. Literacy leadership at its most basic is concerned with one's ability to mentor teachers to achieve their instructional goals. Interpersonal, ethical communication is key to helping teachers achieve their goals.

Cultivate Your Leadership Skills

1. How do Janet's comments about ethical communication connect with and overlap

some of the ideas about communication presented in this chapter?

2. What frustrations are evident in the sample unethical e-mail messages in this feature? How might each leader have expressed his or her frustrations more effectively?

3. The e-mails presented in this feature were all, obviously, forms of written communication. How might these messages have been perceived if they were expressed orally in face-to-face conversations instead of in writing?

Critical Voices

Delivering the Hard Message

—DAWN WENZEL

Dawn is an elementary teacher who works as a network team specialist for the Norwich City school district in New York. She also works with students and teachers in grades K–5 as a classroom coach.

Being a leader sometimes means you have to deliver the hard message. Being a literacy leader is no different. Sometimes delivering the message can cause conflict, but if the issue is handled in a reflective way, and the message is one that truly needs to be delivered, the conflict can be resolved.

As a new network team specialist (NTS), part of my role is to roll out the new Common Core State Standards. This is done during staff development days and collaborative time. My other major role as an NTS is being a coach, both in literacy and math. Surprisingly to me, these two roles came into conflict with one another during the very first staff development day I facilitated.

Our network team comprises three staff members: me, an elementary teacher and literacy specialist; a high school social studies teacher; and the director of curriculum and staff development. We have designed a three-year plan to meet the state mandates regarding the Common Core, as well as meeting our district's needs. Our focus this year is on nonfiction writing. Before we could start our important work around nonfiction writing, however, we first needed to introduce the reasons for and research behind the new Common Core.

This all-important first job was done on our very first staff development day in September. Being that there are four buildings in our district, and only three NTSs, the decision was made to divide and conquer the work that needed to be done. My role was delivering the presentation introducing the Common Core and the research behind it to the staff of our two elementary buildings. The presentation, created by the network team, was to be delivered to all faculty members on the same day. It was important to us that everyone receive the same message at the same time.

The network team had discussed and prepared for anticipated misunderstandings and even disagreements. That, however, did not prepare me for what happened that day. About 40 minutes into my presentation, I showed a slide that listed some of the many reasons the Common Core was developed. I talked about how the Common Core was research based and the consortium looked at countries that have regularly outscored the United States on standardized tests. I mentioned Singapore as one such country—it seemed innocent enough.

From the audience a colleague asked why we should be compared to Singapore when we don't teach in Singapore. I assured my colleague that it wasn't just our state adopting the Common Core, but rather 45 states. The next question came about closing the gap for students who are not on grade level. This is where I said it—this one line that caused this conflict. I said, quoting something I had heard Ken Slentz, deputy commissioner at NYSED, say in an earlier speech, "A great teacher can overcome any gap." And the crowd went wild.

So, now I have just alienated myself from the colleagues whom I will be coaching. I have just angered the very staff with whom I am trying to build a trusting, open relationship. How will I be accepted into their classes as a classroom coach when what they heard, even though not intended, was that they were not great teachers? How can I make them understand that my intent was to express the importance that everyone do everything they can to be the best they can be? How do I undo the message they heard—"No one here is a great teacher"—and replace it with the intended message: "We are great teachers— we just need to be sure we all do the best we can do all the time"?

Sixty-plus staff members, including two administrators, waited to see how I would respond. What could I possibly say that would help me out of this situation? How could I possibly earn their trust? These questions were serious, and I had 4.5 seconds to answer them.

At first, I tried to backtrack and said something along the lines of "Let's forget I ever said that." That was *not* helpful. I then took a deep breath and said that actually I did believe in that statement. I also said that of course we have great teachers in our district and that we need to make sure every child has great teachers in kindergarten, and then first grade, and those great teachers need to continue through every year of that child's schooling. Only if we all strive to be great teachers can we hope to close the gaps.

It's been a few months since that day in September and I am still trying to soothe some of the wounds I inadvertently inflicted. I am still not doing as much classroom coaching as I had hoped to do, but I'm finding a way to help where and when I can. Recently, I approached a teacher to offer some classroom coaching and the response I received, "We'll have to wait until after the holidays," and the refusal to confirm a specific date to meet, told me that the wounds are still healing, slowly. I will, however, be coaching in a classroom not far from that classroom. My colleague, whom I have worked with before, has asked me back to his room to provide him feedback on some changes he has made. I hope my presence there will send the message that I'm really not the enemy, but rather someone who loves to work collaboratively with others to help make *us* the best teachers we can possibly be.

As a reflective practitioner, I can clearly see why my words were hard to hear. I understand how the intention of those words was lost as people took the statement personally. I know now to be mindful of how the words you say may be misinterpreted. I have also learned, however, that sometimes the message itself is a hard one, but the message still must be delivered. Finding this balance may, truly, be the most challenging part of my job. Only time will tell.

Cultivate Your Leadership Skills

1. Using the suggestions from this chapter, compose a response that might have helped Dawn better express her intended message.
2. Why were Dawn's words hard for the teachers to hear?
3. Can you think of a situation that you've had that is similar to this one? How did you handle the situation? What did you learn from that experience?

Questions for Reflection and Discussion

1. With which types of communication do you feel most confident? What do you see as your strengths in this type of communication?

2. With which types of communication do you feel least confident? What do you see as your needs? How might you improve your confidence or skills so you feel more confident?

3. This chapter provides many specific examples and ideas for improving communication as a literacy leader. Which points will be most valuable to you? Describe how you will apply what you learned from this chapter to your role and situation.

4. Read Case Scenario A. What is the most ethical way for Rita to communicate with the administrator, the school board, and the teachers in this situation? She wants to avoid an "us-versus-them" paradigm that pits teachers and administrators against each other with her in the middle. She wants to advocate for the teachers by helping them to find and express their voices and concerns in a proactive way. What should she do?

Case Scenario A

Rita is an elementary literacy leader. She has been asked by her administrator and the school board to focus on choosing a new literature-based reading program. Teachers in Grades 1 through 4 will be required to use the new program as their core reading program beginning in September of the next school year.

This directive does not meet with Rita's philosophy of teaching reading. Having talked with several teachers, she knows many will be resistant to this change. One teacher told her in confidence, "You know they won't change their minds on this. Let's just order a program and they'll never know what we're doing with it in our classrooms."

5. Coming full circle, reread the Chinese proverb with which this chapter begins. Now that you've read and reflected on this chapter, as a literacy leader, how would you most effectively share what the tongue can speak or the eyes cannot see?

Practical Applications

How might this chapter apply to your teaching context and experience? Try these activities:

Classroom Activity

Sometimes the authors think our own children (and even sometimes our husbands!) speak a different language than we do. You say one thing, and they hear something totally different. Or, they say something and we're lost in the popular culture or daily experiences of their world to which we aren't privy. Did you ever get that feeling with your students? Take a day or two to closely observe and listen to how your students communicate. Note what factors determine or cause effective communication and miscommunications. Then, think about or talk with a friend about how, as their teachers, you can better hear what your students are saying.

Professional Development Activity

Create a workshop as an opportunity to disseminate information, model effective communication, and create shared learning experiences. Include teachers and administrators or solely teachers. Teachers may gather together as grade-level units or perhaps across grades, rallying around one particular topic related to this chapter. Include the following components: personal introductions, discussing the agenda as framework for learning, direct instruction, guided practice, reflection, and a closing protocol.

Begin with personal introductions and perhaps a warm-up activity for fun to cultivate an atmosphere of trust, communication, and learning. Participants then move into an introduction to the communication topic grounded in research and rationale, followed by a demonstration of the communication skill with critical reflection afterward. This demonstration may be a model dialogue with workshop participants only, a model conversation in a classroom conducted by the teacher/leader or coach, or perhaps a video or Web clip of a particular communication scenario. After observing, participants reflect upon the communication in preparation for guided practice.

During guided practice, role play to gain a felt sense of actually implementing proactive communication practices. Depending upon the number of workshop participants, the facilitator may need to set participants up to engage in two or three guided practice sessions during the workshop so participants experience both roles. Guided practice can occur in the workshop space or a classroom with students. During guided practice, the literacy leader supports participants through praise and proactive, in-the-moment feedback.

Afterward, facilitate a closing/debriefing so participants have the time and space to reflect upon what they learned, evaluate their own performance, and create an action plan for further inquiry and learning. Collaboratively, set the next agenda.

References

Anderson, L. W., & Krathwohl, D. R. (Eds.). (2001). *A taxonomy for learning, teaching, and assessing: A revision of Bloom's taxonomy of educational objectives: Complete edition.* New York: Longman.

Auerbach, R. (n.d.). Retrieved from http://www.developingteachers.com/quotes/q1.htm

Beebe, S., Beebe, S., & Redmond, M. (2005). *Interpersonal communication: Relating to others* (5th ed.). Boston: Pearson.

Bloom, B. S., & Krathwohl, D. R. (1956). *Taxonomy of educational objectives: The classification of educational goals by a committee of college and university examiners. Handbook 1: Cognitive domain.* New York: Longman.

Brookfield, S. D., & Preskill, S. (2005). *Discussion as a way of teaching: Tools and techniques for democratic classrooms.* San Francisco, CA: Jossey-Bass.

Calkins, L., Ehrenworth, M., & Lehman, C. (2012). *Pathways to the Common Core: Accelerating achievement.* Portsmouth, NH: Heinemann.

Clark, R., & Ivanic, R. (1997). *The politics of writing.* New York: Routledge.

Ekman, P. (2000). *Telling lies: Clues to deceit in the marketplace, politics, and marriage.* New York: W. W. Norton.

Hamlin, S. (2006). *How to talk so people listen: Connecting in today's workplace.* New York: Collins.

Johnston, P. (2004). *Choice words: How our language affects children's learning.* Portland, ME: Stenhouse Publishers.

Richards, J., Bennett, S., & Shea, K. (2007). Making meaning of graduate students' and preservice teachers' e-mail communication in a community of practice. *The Qualitative Report, 12*(4), 639–657. Retrieved from http://www.nova.edu/ssss/QR/QR12-4/richards.pdf

Silverman, D. (2000). Analyzing talk and text. In N. K. Denzin & Y. S. Lincoln (Eds.), *Handbook of qualitative research* (2nd ed., pp. 821–834). Thousand Oaks, CA: Sage.

Shaw, G. B. (n.d.). Retrieved from http://www.plainlanguage.gov/resources/quotes/historical.cfm

Wheatley, M. J. (2002). *Turning to one another: Simple conversations to restore hope to the future.* San Francisco, CA: Berrett-Koehler Publishers.

6

Innovating a Mosaic of Creative Change

> ❝ *I took your advice and managed to make some quite good things out of paintings I considered irredeemable.* ❞
>
> —CLAUDE MONET

Introduction

We begin this chapter with a recent entry from Kristine's teaching journal. She wrote it after reflecting on how Monet's quote relates to what she is working on in her position as a literacy leader. She wrote:

> In this particular 21st-century moment, my mind is busy with several ideas: real-world literacy and social action; creative coaching; transformation; engaging, student-directed classroom practices; and sustainable learning. I have all of these ideas—these desires and visions—of how I wish our classroom to be! But, how do I move from imagination to action? How do I get these ideas out of my head and into the world as something tangible? How do I make this into curriculum, instruction, and assessment? How do I make the change? And, how will it be sustainable?

As a literacy leader, take care and pause for a moment to reflect upon, understand, and empathize with Kristine's moment. Literacy leaders should be able to recognize in her experience one of the hard parts in education—moving past the status quo, moving past a pattern of thinking and behavior that has been in place, whether a short time or a long time. On the surface, we see Kristine trying to figure out her next steps. We can see intention and purpose and philosophy in her thinking and plans for action.

But, in this vignette, what should we make of the subtext? What lies beneath the surface that may be getting in the way of her taking organized action? Only Kristine can truly know—but it is the work of the literacy leader to support her in bringing the subtext to a conscious level. In helping Kristine to dig a bit deeper, we can support her next moves as a literacy leader. For us, thinking about the subtext raises questions like the following:

- Does Kristine believe she is *capable* of organizing these ideas and putting them into action? In this moment, would she benefit by analyzing her strengths and abilities? Might this self-analysis generate the courage and self-esteem needed so she can focus on organizing these ideas into a coherent plan?

- Is Kristine perceiving and/or experiencing structural or environmental circumstances blocking her ability to craft a plan? Is she surmising that time, resources, and/or support is static? Is Kristine about to write off her ideas because she thinks time, resources, and support from administration are rigidly in place—unmovable and inflexible? Would opening this up for conversation create a path for finding a solution?

- To what degree does Kristine's vision reflect clarity? Would Kristine benefit from imaging in greater detail what she is hoping to accomplish? What does she see as the specifics of her plan? Would gaining clarity, sharpening the vision, help to set the next steps in motion?

■ Within Kristine's vision, what is she thinking and feeling that she still needs to learn in terms of content and/or process to be comfortable moving forward? How might further learning help to inspire next steps?

When literacy leaders are working with both surface and subtext, we are surely engaged in cultivating life-enhancing relationships and learning communities. This deeper work is holistic and life-enhancing. It models and engenders respect.

Reflecting back to the opening quote, Monet intentionally frames his thinking and creative process to find the positive in what seems irredeemable. And then, he goes a step further! He pulls forward the positive and uses it to create something new. Let's connect this to Kristine's journaling work. Kristine is surely a literacy leader. Perhaps she is a literacy leader needing support to pull forward the positive as a bridge to creating something new. When Kristine is working with colleagues—other literacy leaders—who understand the power of creative process, she will be able to quickly and effectively access the support she needs through collegial peer conversations, collaborative work, or through dialogue with a supervisor or principal. When the total environment is engaged in creative work, the "what" and "how" of literacy leadership becomes more a matter of honoring, bridging, and connecting. (See how Dawn Hamlin connects the ideas in this chapter to response to intervention in her feature.)

Response to Intervention (RTI) and the Literacy Leader
Tools of the Trade
—DAWN HAMLIN

Dawn is a former special education teacher who has taught in both traditional public schools and residential facilities. She is currently assistant professor at SUNY College at Oneonta.

Literacy leaders working within the RTI framework will need to become familiar and fluent with many "tools of the trade." Critical to the RTI process is the ability to accurately and efficiently collect data and turn it into easily understood graphs for interpretation. Literacy leaders must be familiar with graphing tools and conventions, often with equal-interval charts, and maybe, in some instances, standard celebration charts.

Capturing data may often take place through written assessments, but digital voice recordings may also elicit useful assessment and instructional planning information. How, then, may literacy leaders "capture" data that may be elusive or inconsistent? Think about how often a student may respond to questions or interact with peers in a discussion group—getting at this data can be challenging. In some instances, the educator may use an index card and make check marks for each observed behavior, but in many teaching scenarios this might not be feasible. One good way to capture more unusual academic behaviors would be to use rubber bands or paper clips. These items are easily found in many classrooms and can be used quickly. In one situation where I worked with a student to increase his verbal interactions with peers, I would start the session with a dozen rubber bands on my left arm. As the student commented appropriately in the discussion, I would move a rubber band to the other arm.

At the completion of class I had a "permanent record" that could then be entered into my data collection system and provide accurate, reliable information on how our communication intervention was working. Paper clips could be used as well, transferring them from one pocket to another as the behavior was observed. This form of data capture is rather unobtrusive and will not greatly alter the flow of a lesson, and it will result in much more accurate data than trying to rely on memory alone.

Let's go deeper into this work by exploring the role of creativity as a process in literacy leadership.

Creativity and Literacy Leadership

Throughout the chapters of this book, we have used the terms "create" and "creative" quite a bit without directly addressing "creativity" as a concept that can be applied in our work as literacy leaders. Robinson and Aronica (2009, 2011) suggests that to solve 21st-century global issues, we need to fundamentally transform systems of education. The original design of education and schooling was crafted for particular purposes. But, our current local and global needs have outgrown these purposes. When crafting schooling and mass education for the industrial age, not only was the purpose specific, so too was the kind of thinking upon which the original structure relied—a model of rational, objective, industrial-like sensibilities. But our context is different now. And as a result, our needs are different now.

We live in a time of rapid technological change. Our world is a global network and we are all interconnected through a variety of means. We have quick access to a tremendous amount of information and knowledge. Technology shapes how we live, how we learn, and how we work. Most critical is the realization that technology is shaping the kind of work needed in the world now and in the future. This in turn shapes the kind of education needed to prepare people for present and future employment. It provides a rationale. Both Ken Robinson and Tony Wagner, author of *The Global Achievement Gap: Why Even Our Best Schools Don't Teach the New Survival Skills Our Children Need—and What We Can Do About It* (2008) and *Creating Innovators: The Making of Young People Who Will*

Change the World (2012), explicitly detail the much-needed qualities employers are expecting of potential job candidates:

- Critical *and* creative thinking
- Ability to devise alternative solutions to complex issues
- Entrepreneurial attitude and spirit
- Ability to collaborate in diverse contexts
- Effective communication skills (oral and written)
- Cultural understanding
- Adaptability and responsiveness

Both Robinson and Wagner—and many others—advocate for a shift in the purpose and process of education to best meet the local and global challenges of the 21st century—and beyond. This is why creativity matters—education needs its leaders creating a culture of innovation. In doing so, "to realize our true creative potential—in our organizations, in our schools, and in our communities—we need to think differently about ourselves and to act differently towards each other. We must learn to be creative" (Robinson, 2011, p. 286). We believe literacy leaders are in the unique position to be catalysts in creating cultures of innovation! But how?

Robinson identifies three purposes for schooling: personal, cultural, and economic. Literacy leaders are certainly able to advocate for and design learning experiences to nurture personal development, advocate for a deepening of how we understand the world, and facilitate skill development as preparation for the world of work. Literacy leaders are doing this through the new Common Core State Standards, so let's make it public! (Read this chapter's connection to the Common Core State Standards Connection by Tracey Johnson.) Let's be intentional and acknowledge that this is why we are nurturing the development of all learners—colleagues and students with whom we work. Let's also advocate "teaching for creativity" as Robinson so aptly describes. Balancing skill development and exploring ideas, literacy leaders

- nurture the creative spirit and abilities of colleagues and students;
- strategize with others to form dynamic professional learning communities whereby participants are working with other colleagues who value diversity, critical thinking, and learning in ways that challenge individuals to grow beyond their own status quo;
- model and encourage innovative thinking;
- advocate inquiry through open-ended questioning, helping colleagues and students to learn to ask their own big questions;
- generate solutions through imagination, creativity, and innovation;
- advocate learning for the future and the here and now, modeling how to live and work fully present in the current moment.

Literacy leadership is a creative endeavor.

The Common Core State Standards Connection

Involvement and Influence in Planning Change

—TRACEY JOHNSON

Tracey currently works at the New York State Education Department. She has over 22 years of teaching experience, including serving as a literacy coordinator at the Capital Region Board of Cooperative Educational Services (BOCES), an adjunct professor at Sage Graduate School in Troy, New York, and an ELA Coordinator/Reading First Coach in a charter school.

The adoption of the Common Core Standards has brought on a shift in expectations for the education community at large. Teachers need supports to develop their own interpretation of what to teach and how to teach it. As a person of influence, the literacy leader has to reflect on his or her own interpretations and make recommendations based on mutual understandings of what teachers need and are expected to fulfill. The key is to be a positive influence. These shifts may arouse uncomfortable feelings because of the higher-level comprehension and analytical reading skills emphasized. However, if you are a person who sees hope and opportunity, you can make a difference.

Six shifts in ELA/literacy curricular materials and classroom instruction are required to ensure alignment to the Common Core Standards. Shifts 1 and 2 require students to read more informational texts instead of referring to them. The expectation is that students will access world science, social studies, the arts, and literature through text. Shifts 3 and 4 encourage teachers to spend more time on close and careful reading of complex text around which instruction is centered. To assess comprehension of the complex text, students provide text-based answers, both in conversation and in writing. Shifts 5 and 6 emphasize writing arguments that respond to the ideas, facts, and arguments presented in the texts they read and developing academic vocabulary that is rich and domain specific.

Across the text thus far, we have been advocating for a change in how literacy leadership is understood, experienced, and practiced in the field. It is important to keep in mind the tangible strategies that literacy leaders can fold into their work as practical applications. We positioned the following strategies (applications) as critical to literacy leadership:

- Democratic processes and shared leadership
- Systems thinking
- Linking purpose, philosophy, and practice
- Nurturing and celebrating growth, learning, and development
- Narrative inquiry
- Appreciative leadership and coaching

- Creating networked learning communities
- Teachers as leaders designing their own professional learning
- Applying key principles of adult learning—andragogy
- Critical and collaborative communication
- Applying imagination, creativity, and innovation
- Implementing RTI and the Common Core

Breathing life into these strategies is a courageous act! Folding imagination, creativity, and innovation into our work as literacy leaders is a noble and much-needed endeavor. By doing so, we can ignite energy and enthusiasm for learning. We will be able to imagine, create, and innovate new ways of working to enhance the learning for ourselves, our colleagues, and our students with whom we work. This deeper work of folding imagination, creativity, and innovation into our literacy leadership is an emergent process, and we need examples of change in progress and portraits of creativity in action to serve as sources of promise and possibility for our literacy-leadership work.

We turn our attention now to one such source of promise and possibility—a portrait of Ridge and Valley Charter School in Blairstown, New Jersey.

Imagination, Creativity, and Innovation in Action at Ridge and Valley Charter School

As literacy leaders, we look to professional books, current research, colleagues, workshops, and our own creativity, imagination, and innovation for strategies to improve our performance and understanding of literacy-leadership work. We also learn through mentoring and coaching. In crafting a portrait of Ridge and Valley Charter School (RVCS), we hope that you will learn by example. We hope that this portrait of Ridge and Valley serves as a mentor or coach or guide offering additional insight and strategies to enhance how we envision and practice literacy leadership. But that's not all. This portrait is also an invitation to rethink the purpose of school and how learning can be designed to create deep change.

Ridge and Valley Charter School is an example of imagination, creativity, and innovation in action. As a whole, RVCS embodies what Edmund O'Sullivan, a leader in the field of adult learning, calls "visionary transformative education" and "creative transformative learning." He defines this work as "education for planetary consciousness, for integral development, for quality of life, and education and the sacred" (O'Sullivan, Morrell, & O'Connor, 2002, p. 6). Ridge and Valley Charter School has much to share in mission and vision, learning, leadership, and living.

We posed several questions to Traci Pannullo, Lisa Masi, and Kasey Errico—guides/teachers at Ridge and Valley who each play different roles in the design, integration, and implementation of literacy leadership in their school. You will find our questions in bold type; the team's collaborative responses are in italics.

How does the structure of Ridge and Valley Charter School leadership in its entirety promote literacy learning and leadership?

The founders of Ridge and Valley Charter School envisioned our school as a place to reinvent the human presence on our planet—learning and working together in ways that are more respectful and harmonious with the natural world and each other. Our intention, focused through our clear mission statement, is to create and model effective, holistic, and humane systems that question traditional assumptions and offer mutually enhancing solutions. Expecting that all members of our community are lifelong learners, and to support the assumption that everyone has something to offer and something to learn, we work to create student and adult systems that are aligned and mirror one another. One of these foundational systems is our school-wide collaborative governance model that values every voice and encourages input from all perspectives. In this model, which is consistent from our classrooms to our public trustee meetings, leadership is shared and the group meets in circle to allow for the greatest level of equality and engagement. It is in these collaborative circle meetings that participants analyze and synthesize the information they have learned, pose creative solutions, and take action to make change. Participation in this process inherently requires a deeper level of literacy in which students, staff, trustees, and parents understand our mission, current ecological/political/cultural relationships and events, historic responses, state and national academic standards, alternative educational philosophies, pedagogical and ecological literacy, current research and data, mental models, and unintended consequences in order to make well-informed decisions that clearly tie back to our mission and move us toward our common purpose. Each individual, regardless of age or background, is invited to contribute expertise, knowledge, skills, and perspective to the circle, looking for connections and philosophical and statistical support for decisions, within an understanding of our mission context. We are always working to articulate what we are doing and connect why we are doing it to our common mission.

How is professional development organized so that it honors the adult learner?

Professional development at Ridge and Valley utilizes our collaborative model and provides many opportunities for staff to work together in a variety of configurations based upon need. Staff, called "guides" to indicate their more facilitation-based role with the students, express their professional development needs through individual professional development plans and goals, individually and/or collectively during circle meetings, through the process of peer and/or leadership-team observations, and individually to other staff who have expertise in that area or can help them to fulfill those goals and needs. Our small staff, weekly collaborative meetings (individual, team, and/or whole staff), and flexible schedule enable us to meet outside requirements and internal student needs, while being responsive to the emergent needs expressed by staff members. The needs and goals of the guides then inform small and/or whole-group in-house professional development content and experiences. These experiences, which all strongly support peer learning, solicit expertise from within the group, share practical applications and solutions, allow time to practice and apply new skills, celebrate successes, and include peer critique and review. Our guide portfolio system, which mirrors our student portfolio system, encourages feedback and reflection, and provides a place to document achievements. Additionally, our adult learners are honored through our support of external professional development experiences that enhance their mission-based passions, and subsequently through the desire for them to share those passions and expertise with the rest of the staff and students. This system creates an ongoing feedback loop that guides us toward continual improvement.

How is experiential education /experiential learning a vital link to literacy learning?

Literacy learning, like most other learning, is naturally embedded in the real world and is therefore inherently experiential. At RVCS we strive to make all learning as "real life" as possible by engaging students in curricula and learning experiences that are based in authentic, real-world situations, problems, and issues. These experiences require students to actively apply skills and knowledge in ways that are personally meaningful and create change. By moving out of an objective, fragmented, mechanistic approach to the world and into a more organic, dynamic, subjective interaction with the situation, problem, or issue at hand, we cultivate deeper levels of care and personal engagement, and a greater investment in outcomes. By using a project-based learning model, we investigate interdisciplinary system-based issues that are relevant to students and, when possible, individualize these through student interest and choice. These projects require an understanding of content and context, support multiple intelligences, incorporate teamwork and collaborative thinking, require synthesis, and help students make connections. Without experiencing literacy skills as a living process and applying them in authentic projects, the skills themselves can seem like simply detached bits of information.

For example, at the beginning of each year, each class group selects a class name based on a bioregional organism category, such as trees. The guides and students use the circle process to discuss the category, research and write about bioregional organisms (and their characteristics) in that category, determine which organism has the qualities that they feel best represent them as a group, and then use consensus decision making to decide on their class group name. Each class group then works together to design a presentation on their class name and the organism, and then shares it with the whole school at our weekly school assembly. For the rest of the year, that class group and the students in it are referred to by that name. Throughout the process, students are developing and applying skills in literacy and collaboration and having fun, too!

What are a few important professional resources you use to nurture literacy leadership?

The following resources support literacy leadership at RVCS by supporting integrated, interdisciplinary thinking and collaborative, personally engaging processes:

- *Teachers College Reading Writing Project*
- *Collaborative Circle Process and Governance*
- *Ecological Literacy*
- *Interdisciplinary, Project-Based Learning*
- *Professional Learning Communities*

How is communication at Ridge and Valley proactive, critical, and collaborative?

Communication at RVCS is a living, ongoing process that expects personal responsibility and participation from each person. Our collaborative circle process, use of nonviolent communication practices and "I" statements, and consensus decision making contribute to a culture that asks each person to offer what they can and ask for what they need. Daily class circles and weekly guide circles allow communication to flow in a timely manner, as anyone can bring up a concern or celebrate a success at any time. Our check-in process at the beginning of each circle allows for personalized interactions and experiences, deepens relationships and empathy, and gives others insights into forces that might be impacting the person or group that day. Additionally, through our behavior rubric, Medicine Wheel behavioral system, and our Core Values, we have articulated the personal behaviors and positive relationships we expect from our community members.

How does your school mission and vision drive literacy learning and leadership?

Ridge and Valley's mission and culture of inquiry require that our work and learning together are infused with literacy. Through our curriculum framework, Project-Based Learning, and experiential education, our students build bioregional awareness and confidence that translates to all learning. Our curriculum framework (which organizes content into interdisciplinary, ecologically based lenses), our scope and sequence of key learning experiences (which ensure consistency of experiential, mission-based learning across the grades), and our multiage team-teaching approach within multiyear curriculum loops (which supports the development of long-term relationships between students, parents, and guides) creates an environment in which literacy learning and leadership take center stage. Literacy is critical to the investigation, analysis, defense, synthesis, and representation of all other content, and strength in this area—by the students and the adults—facilitates rich, vibrant learning that is alive and emergent.

How is literacy learning/literacy leadership assessed and celebrated?

Literacy is assessed at RVCS in a variety of formal and informal ways. We not only utilize traditional assessments (such as standardized testing, in-house diagnostic assessments, and assessments that reflect the Common Core), but also authentic assessments that are the result of real-world projects in which students synthesize content into proactive solutions, community actions, and presentations. Throughout the school year, guides and students are given frequent opportunities for reflecting on and showcasing their work and growth: at our weekly assembly; during student-led conferences with parents; during the peer critique process; at our yearend Celebration of Learning; within student- and guide-written narrative reflections for student/staff portfolios and our whole student reports (report cards); through students' independent study projects; and, for staff, through the sharing of expertise and successes highlighted through team, whole circle, and professional development collaborations. At the end of the day, the ultimate measure of our literacy leadership success occurs every day as the adults all work on the real-world challenge of running an alternative school within the confines of a traditional educational structure, while creating student learning experiences that provide that same type of application of their literacy and knowledge to real-world problems and issues that are relevant to them.

Powerful, creative, and transformative! We would like to extend our thanks to Traci Pannullo, Lisa Masi, and Kasey Errico for their inspiring contribution.

Let's take a moment to reflect upon the content of this portrait to consider how we are influenced as literacy leaders. Learning and leadership strategies used at Ridge and Valley that are of benefit to all literacy leaders include the following:

■ Clarity of mission and vision, core values, and foundation principles
■ Holistic and humane systems thinking
■ Lifelong learning
■ Alignment of student and adult systems
■ Collaborative governance model and circle meetings
■ Shared expertise, knowledge, skills, and perspectives
■ Guide/facilitation roles
■ Individual and collective professional development plans
■ Flexible scheduling
■ Portfolio systems
■ On-site and external professional development
■ Embedded, real-world literacy practices
■ Interdisciplinary, project-based learning

- Shared resources
- Collaborative communication
- Multiage team-teaching approach/curricular loops
- Experiential education/experiential learning
- Authentic assessments
- Celebration of learning

As literacy leaders, which strategies do you already use in your local context? Which strategies would you like to share with colleagues and students where you work?

Ridge and Valley Charter School is a wonderful example of life-enhancing learning and leading. We can see how imagination, creativity, and innovation are *possible* and *essential* to our work as educators in the field. We can see how learning and leadership are layered, complex, and creatively emerge over time. RVCS has much to offer in purpose, philosophy, and pedagogy. To learn more about RVCS, please explore its website at http://ridgeandvalley.org.

Closing Thoughts

In this chapter, we explored the ways in which literacy leadership is a creative process. Like Sir Ken Robinson, we too propose imagination, creativity, and innovation as ways of thinking and being that hold the potential to bring forth a new purpose and process of education—a purpose and process that is life enhancing for the present and life enhancing for possible futures. Ridge and Valley Charter School offered us a portrait of promise and possibility for literacy leadership and creative transformation.

Literacy learning and leadership are creative processes. The essence of our work is experienced as imagination, creativity, and innovation. As literacy leaders, we are stewards in creating life-enhancing learning communities and learning experiences to nourish the hearts, minds, and souls of the colleagues and students with whom we work. Literacy leadership is the cultivation of creativity and deep learning.

Next, we invite you to hear voices of more literacy leaders in the field as you read and contemplate The Ethical Literacy Leader and Critical Voices features in this chapter. Following each feature are questions in the Cultivate Your Leadership Skills section to prompt your thinking as you work toward innovating a mosaic of creative change in your context. To read more about the contributors' backgrounds, see the About the Contributors section.

The Ethical Literacy Leader

Advocating for a Model of Equity

—SHERRY DISMUKE AND ROBIN SLY

Sherry is a classroom teacher who has served as the cochair of her school RTI committee. She teaches literacy classes and supervises teacher candidates for Boise State University.

Robin is the 2009 Idaho State Teacher of the Year. She is a classroom teacher who is currently serving as the chair of her school RTI committee.

A few years ago, our roles as first-grade teachers were expanded as we took on the added responsibilities of coordinating our school's implementation of a response to intervention (RTI) model. We discovered the best way to meet all students' and teachers' needs and expectations has been to adopt a collaborative, problem-solving model that upholds the ethical values in which our district believes. We have found RTI to be an inclusive and equitable way to meet the needs of learners.

Through the RTI model, schools and districts may decide to address the needs of their students with a one-size-fits-all protocol model or a collaborative, problem-solving model. For our district, this became an ethical and philosophical decision.

As we understood it, the protocol model requires the RTI team to prescribe the same standardized academic interventions for all students, including struggling students with scores below benchmarks, without regard for individual learning needs. In contrast, the problem-solving model relies on a professional learning community to evaluate and analyze the effectiveness of the school's overall curriculum and the ability to deliver differentiated solutions. These negotiated solutions take into consideration a child's environmental, social, emotional, and academic needs. Plans are made jointly with those who know the child best, and teams are given authority to remove institutional barriers to access solutions.

After thoroughly investigating the prescriptive practices of a protocol model, we stood firm for the adoption of a model that would continually question teaching practices and the environment of a child first, before making judgments about a child's ability to learn.

Teachers have been indoctrinated in a system that has taught us to turn to testing when our teaching methods fail. In our new role as teacher leaders, we have learned to deny our initial impulse to jump straight to testing and to, instead, question our own teaching. Our problem-solving team is learning to collaboratively seek out new, more effective teaching and assessment practices to target students' specific difficulties. This work has improved teacher practice and has successfully scaffolded student learning. Many struggling students have made gains without labels or the need for extensive testing.

Literacy leaders on RTI teams must also guard against another possible abuse of RTI. Districts could be tempted to see RTI as a way to exclude many children from the expert services they deserve and need. With qualification more difficult, inexperienced problem-solving teams run the risk of underqualifying students in need. Both remediation and acceleration can be withheld until teams become proficient at this new process. Literacy leaders need to advocate for careful recordkeeping of all inquiries and the monitoring of their progress.

For most teacher leaders, there has been nothing in our preservice teacher education or teacher professional development that has adequately prepared us for our new roles in RTI. However, we must be diligent now in making ourselves experts at not only collaboration and inquiry, but also the ever-changing forms, procedures, and protocols of RTI if we are going to advocate for the rights of all children to be served.

Following are eight reasons why we believe RTI offers more equitable solutions for students and teachers:

1. RTI invites teachers, parents, and students to be part of the solution instead of assuming they are part of the problem.
2. RTI looks first at changing the learning environment to provide solutions before assuming struggling children have learning disabilities.
3. RTI is more equitable than the old discrepancy model in which students first had to fail before qualifying for services.
4. RTI is dependent upon the collaboration and expertise of all team members. Each team member has an equal voice and shared accountability.

5. Second-language learners can receive literacy intervention without having to be labeled "learning disabled."
6. Learners in need of acceleration in one or more areas can be paired with appropriate strategies and talent development without having to meet the IQ requirements set by their district.
7. RTI focuses on differentiated instruction to meet the needs of all learners.
8. All students are still provided access to the core curriculum.

Cultivate Your Leadership Skills

1. How does this feature embody the use of imagination, creativity, and innovation?
2. How does Sherry and Robin's work engage literacy leaders?
3. Does Sherry and Robin's work reflect experiential education/experiential learning and literacy leadership? Explain.
4. Sherry and Robin write: "In our new role as teacher leaders, we have learned to deny our initial impulse to jump straight to testing and to, instead, question our own teaching." Reflect and comment on what this passage means to you and to literacy leadership.

Critical Voices
Encouraging Teachers to Embrace Connectedness
—KATHLEEN MUIR

Kathleen is currently the literacy coach at Cotee River Elementary School in Pasco County, Florida.

Many artists paint a school's canvas. Every person's brush stroke adds layers to the landscape. As an elementary teacher and curriculum design–team chair, I realized that my brush strokes were broader than most because I always look at the "big picture" first.

This put me in the minority at my school. Most of my colleagues were focused on each individual subject area. They worked within the lines of their lesson plan boxes. Reading and math were planned extensively, leaving the content areas of social studies and science glossed over. Complicating this was a new reading series that was to be used with fidelity during the mandated 90-minute reading block. It was a constant struggle to fit everything in.

As a result, I became an advocate for the content areas of social studies and science. At the elementary level, the content areas are not given the attention nor time allotment needed for students to become fully engaged with new concepts. They are usually relegated to the end of the day, "if we can get to it," and most times are given 30 minutes or less. Compounding this is the "they will get that in middle school so why worry about it now" perception of many pressed-for-time elementary teachers. This is understandable in light of the emphasis on accountability measured by high-stakes standardized tests like our Florida Comprehensive Achievement Test (FCAT) that measures mastery of state standards in reading, writing, math, and, most recently, science.

Testing in science has brought it into the foreground and placed it close to reading and math as a priority. Unfortunately, social studies has been left behind (Jones & Thomas, 2006). It is overlooked, a shadow in the background barely visible in the expansive panorama. But not by me! I love reading about history and discovering the connectedness of events past and present. As events in history unfold, patterns are revealed that influence present and future events. Careful examination of and reflection on these patterns help students think critically about their impact on society (Jones & Thomas, 2006).

Critical thinking is an extension of basic reading skills and should begin as early as possible. As a multiage (Grades 3 to 5)

elementary teacher, I was continually impressed with discussions I would have with my students about complex topics. The catalysts for these discussions were picture books I shared as part of whole-group instruction. The purpose of whole-group instruction was to introduce a reading skill or strategy. The books were selected based on the particular skill or strategy presented, not on the content information. The discussions shared sometimes would eclipse the reading strategy, but the engagement and interaction were remarkable. I began to wonder how I could find the connectedness between the content and the reading skills and strategies.

The answer to me was clear but complex. A connected curriculum presented in layers like a fine oil painting but updated to appeal to the multimedia age was required. A different take on a familiar thematic approach long abandoned could work. I began to sketch the first layer of my plan. I drew lines. My lines turned into boxes for social studies, science, and reading. I made charts of the standards, essential questions, reading skills, reading strategies, picture books, and textbooks. I spoke to fellow teachers, most notably Nikki Rodriguez. I presented my ideas to my principal, Kathy Rushe, and my reading specialist, Faye Matadobra. They both supported my ideas and gave me the green light.

I developed a curriculum map for one quarter of the school year that led with the social studies and science requirements outlined by the district. I used a content-centric approach with reading skills and strategies embedded and high-quality, content-related picture books as the medium. Nikki helped with the selection of science picture books and mapped out the science piece. Rhoda, the media specialist, made book suggestions. Faye helped me align the reading standards with skills and strategies for each picture book.

Kathy approved the purchase of the selected books. I then presented my plan to the staff.

I would like to say it was met with cheers and applause. It wasn't! In retrospect, I think there were many reasons for this. First and foremost are the pressures in this age of accountability that leave educators leery of anything that is perceived as new, done before and failed, or perceived as a paradigm shift. Second, I did not understand the professional development required. I assumed because I was passionate about this and could see the connectedness so clearly, others would share my vision. I thought that if I write it, they will come. Many did not. I can't say I wasn't disappointed.

My principal, Kathy, assured me that change would take time and I needed to be patient. She said that people need time to process information, question it, and try it out before they are willing to embrace it fully. She advised me to take baby steps. It was then that I realized the complexities of being a school administrator and the importance of staff development. Kathy advocated for my ideas, but needed to consider *her* big picture at Trinity. She worked at developing her staff at Trinity and was proud of the talented ensemble. I realized I needed to take the next step myself. I decided to continue my education and become a reading coach.

As a student seeking a master's degree in reading at the University of South Florida, I was required to develop a curriculum plan. The connectedness of my two worlds, work and school, was never more clear. Content literacy and integrated curriculum became my focus. As with everything I do, I wanted this to be something that would benefit my students in the classroom. My recent experience made it clear that I would have to be sure that the curriculum was connected *and* accountable. The instructional plan needed to be accountable to the standards,

the teachers, and, more important, the students.

Dr. Nancy Williams, my graduate advisor and friend from the University of South Florida, calls this "affective accountability." Affective accountability is a process that extends effective teaching to include motivation, enjoyment, accomplishment, and self-worth, and offers an instructional plan that honors all children's right to excellent reading instruction (Williams & Bauer, 2006). With this in mind, I developed an instructional plan for the next school year. I spoke more about the process of developing the plan with the teachers and supported it with research. I presented the plan at staff-development meetings and solicited input on picture books, materials, activities, and so forth from the staff. I formed a committee to align the reading and content standards to each picture book. We examined the reading series and determined where we could best fit each chapter. Teachers volunteered to come in over the summer to organize materials. We were ready for the school year.

I would love to say that everyone embraced the connected curriculum and we had an outstanding year. Our students did extremely well; however, I cannot say with all certainty that it was because the curriculum plan was used as intended. Teachers selected what they wanted and understood—bits and pieces of the whole that in my mind was an abstract of what was intended. As I learned more and more about coaching, I realized that the resistance came not from an unwillingness to cooperate, but from a reluctance to change educational beliefs. Like looking at a fine work of art, everyone sees something different depending upon his or her perspective and is entitled to an opinion. Just as we differentiate for students, staff-development experiences need to consider the differing philosophies of teachers (Kise, 2006).

My educational landscape is still developing. I stepped back to examine the shades and shadows and continue to add layers of understanding. I am currently the K–12 literacy coach at Dr. John Long Middle School. The staff development this year is centered on the Common Core Standards. The Common Core Standards take an integrated approach to teaching and learning that incorporates a broadened view of literacy necessary for our students to be competitive in college and careers (National Governors Association Center for Best Practices, Council of Chief State School Officers, 2010). Additionally, I am working with Dr. Williams on a transdisciplinary approach to curriculum that centers on the transfer of knowledge between content areas and, more important, between teachers and students. I am excited about what is to come and hope that my masterpiece is never finished.

Cultivate Your Leadership Skills

1. How do Kathleen's experiences connect with the themes presented in this chapter?
2. How else might Kathleen approach this situation, applying imagination, creativity, and innovation? Would teachers react differently? In what ways? Why or Why not?
3. In what ways did Kathleen seek to improve her skills as a literacy leader?

Questions for Reflection and Discussion

1. Which literacy-leadership strategies resonate with you? Which ones would you like to learn more about? Why?

2. What does cultivating a culture of innovation look like in your mind and your local context? How might you collaborate with others to build a mission and vision supporting this work?

3. Compare your school mission, vision, and leadership strategies to those of Ridge and Valley Charter School. What is the positive that already exists in your context? What would you like to innovate anew?

4. In what ways is the RTI system impacting literacy education and literacy leadership? Is experiential, holistic, authentic, and deep learning evidenced across the RTI system? Is this true for students and adults participating in the system?

5. How does your interpretation of the Common Core Standards reflect teaching for creativity?

6. Coming full circle, reread Monet's quote that begins this chapter. Now that you've read and reflected on this chapter, how do you see Monet's words connecting to literacy leadership and cultivating cultures of innovation?

Practical Applications

How might this chapter apply to your teaching context and experience? Try these activities:

Classroom Activity

How might you connect literacy to community development and social action? Plan a community mapping activity with your students. Demonstrate how to map neighborhoods, organizations, and businesses. Imagine how literacy is used in a variety of community contexts. Model a variety of ways that students can use literacy to research community issues and needs. Teach students how to plan and implement local projects where literacy is in service of a larger cause/project.

Professional Development Activity

In collaboration with colleagues, apply the principles of appreciative leadership and appreciative coaching to explore the role of imagination, creativity, and innovation in your local context. Share stories, create a vision, and craft a plan for the next steps in your growth and development, and the growth and development of the students with whom you work. Celebrate success!

References

Jones, R., & Thomas, T. (2006). Leave no discipline behind. *The Reading Teacher, 60*(1), 58–64.

Kise, J. A. (Ed.). (2006). *Differentiated coaching: A framework for helping teachers change.* Corwin Press.

National Governors Association Center for Best Practices, Council of Chief State School Officers. (2010). *Common core state standards.* Washington, DC: National Governors Association Center for Best Practices, Council of Chief State School Officers.

O'Sullivan, E., Morrell, A., & O'Connor, M. A. (2002). (Eds.). *Expanding the boundaries of transformative learning.* New York: Palgrave.

Ridge and Valley Charter School. (n.d.). http://ridgeandvalley.org/

Robinson, K., & Aronica, L. (2009). *The element: How finding your passion changes everything.* New York: Penguin Books.

Robinson, K. (2011). *Out of our minds: Learning to be creative.* West Susses, United Kingdom: Capstone

Wagner, T. (2008). *The global achievement gap: Why even our best schools don't teach the new survival skills our children need—and what we can do about it.* New York: Basic Books.

Williams, N., & Bauer, P. (2006). Pathways to affective accountability: Selecting, locating, and using children's books in elementary classrooms. *The Reading Teacher, 60*(1), 14–22.

Texturing with Resources

> 66 *As soon as you can, place yourself under the guidance of a master, and remain with him as long as possible.* 99
>
> —CENNINO CENNINI

Introduction

Cennini's quote implies an artist will benefit and perhaps even flourish under the tutelage of a "master" artist. Is the same true for literacy leaders and others in the field of literacy education? We believe so! This chapter is all about reaching out to others: other people, organizations, publications, technology, and any imaginable resource that will help us grow and develop as knowledgeable literacy leaders.

Technology and collaborative resources in the professional arena are evolving so quickly that by the time you read this chapter, hundreds or even thousands of new ideas and resources will have emerged out of creativity and necessity. The secret is to keep yourself up to date. Read, learn from others, take classes, and learn by experiencing new technologies and ideas. Be open to the possibilities technological advancements bring into the classroom and into your professional development.

Literacy leaders have only begun to tap the power and potential of technology and online resources. Read on to learn about just some of the longstanding and recently fashioned resources currently available to literacy leaders. We'll begin by talking about professional literacy associations and what they have to offer literacy leaders.

The Texture of Professional Literacy Associations

Professional literacy associations offer educators and literacy leaders opportunities for professional development through many avenues, such as

- networking,
- publications,
- conferences,
- resources, and
- webinars,

just to name a few.

We thought it might be helpful for you to see how Cindy's involvement with and reliance upon professional associations progressed over her career as a literacy teacher and leader so you can think about your own professional trajectory. When Cindy was an undergraduate preservice teacher at Plattsburgh State, she joined her first literacy-related professional association—the New York State Reading Association, the state affiliation for the International Reading Association. She didn't become involved at first, but enjoyed receiving and reading the association's journal and attending workshops at its annual conference. As a novice teacher, when she felt more confident that she had something to offer the reading community, she submitted a proposal to present her own workshop at the association's annual conference. The more involved she became in the association, the more knowledgeable and confident she became as an elementary classroom teacher. She met colleagues with similar classroom issues, such as how to best meet the needs of struggling writers and how to prepare her students for the required state assessments in ways that would engage them and strengthen lifelong literacy skills. Through her involvement at the state level, she connected with colleagues who were on committees at the international level. Soon she was chairing a committee and flying off to cities like Chicago and San Antonio to present at workshops and facilitate preconference institutes. Every time she attended a conference or convention, she came back to teaching refreshed, informed, and reflective. She shared new ideas with her colleagues and students.

Moving from involvement at the state level to the international level was a natural transition for Cindy. However, each of us will find and follow our own path through the myriad of options and choices professional associations offer, once we take the first step. Both authors highly recommend membership in a selected professional association or two. But, there are many groups out there. And membership fees can be expensive. How does one decide which association will be the best fit for his or her needs and the needs of the school and students?

The first step is to reflect on what your expectations are for association membership. Do you want membership to include journals about research or evidence-based classroom practices? Do you want to have opportunities to attend local conferences, or do you think it would be more beneficial to attend more widely attended conventions? Do you want to join a particular special-interest group to focus your attention on, perhaps, word study or action research?

We suggest you learn what each literacy professional association has to offer. The appendix at the end of this book offers a listing of a number of literacy professional associations. We have invited current association presidents and leaders to describe how their groups act as literacy leaders and what resources they offer to support literacy leaders. The following associations, listed alphabetically, appear in the appendix:

American Reading Company by Jane Hileman

American Reading Forum by Nance Wilson and Michael French

Association of Literacy Educators and Researchers by Mary Roe, John Smith, and Rob Erwin

International Reading Association by Victoria Risko

Literacy Research Association by Patricia Anders

National Council of Teachers of English by Yvonne Siu-Runjan

Of course, you can also visit the groups' websites (see appendix) for additional information.

The Texture of Online Professional Development and Networking

Many literacy leaders consider teacher professional development to be the keystone to school reform and improved student learning (Dede, 2006). To meet the needs of teachers' busy schedules, limited time, and the economic needs of school districts in what seems to be an era of change, shrinking budgets, and tough choices, the creation of a number of online professional development and networking programs has been stimulated. These approaches draw on literacy experts who are not available to a district locally and would be costly to obtain otherwise. This technology offers teachers the "just-in-time" resources we need (Pace & Terrell, 2011). No teacher or district should feel isolated when the power to tap into knowledge internationally is readily accessible. (Read this chapter's Response to Intervention (RTI) and the Literacy Leader feature by Dawn Hamlin for online resources to help with RTI implementation. Also, see how Tracey Johnson makes connections to the built-in resources in her feature The Common Core State Standards Connection.)

Response to Intervention (RTI) and the Literacy Leader

What's Up Online

—DAWN HAMLIN

Dawn is currently assistant professor at SUNY College at Oneonta. She is a former special education teacher who taught in both traditional public schools and residential facilities.

Resources available online to support literacy leaders and their RTI programs are both abundant and of varying quality. Literacy leaders will have to very carefully screen resources to make sure that they meet evidence-based practice (EBP) standards, which is a critical component of RTI.

One of the first questions that often arises in RTI is how do I know if a practice is evidence based? While there are many opinions out there as to what constitutes a sufficient evidence base, there are some widely accepted articles (read *Exceptional Children* volume 71) and websites such as What Works Clearinghouse (http://ies.ed.gov/ncee/wwc/) that can help in determining if a practice or intervention gets the EBP "seal of approval."

One of the most user-friendly sites with great information on several aspects of RTI, including reading probe generators and graphing "how-to" information and programs, is http://interventioncentral.org. This website is run by Jim Wright, who also wrote the *RTI Toolkit: A Practical Guide for Schools* (2007). His website also has many sections covering good evidence-based practices that literacy leaders can use to support student attainment and achievement.

Other great websites to check out:

National Center on Response to Intervention
 http://www.rti4success.org/
RTI Action Network http://www.rtinetwork.org/

National Dissemination Center for Children
 with Disabilities (NICHCY) http://nichcy.org/
 schools-administrators/rti

The Common Core State Standards Connection

Built-In Resources

—TRACEY JOHNSON

Tracey's career in education spans over 22 years. She has taught at all educational levels, developed curriculum, provided professional development to persistently low-achieving schools, and mentored teachers. She is currently employed at the New York State Education Department.

The Common Core State Standards initiative has considerable implications for our classrooms. The transition from former state standards to the Common Core Standards may present a daunting challenge to teachers, especially during a time when the mandates of federal initiatives and the fiscal climate of our national, state, and local communities are being felt by everyone. In an attempt to provide the tools for teachers to make a smooth transition from previous state standards to the Common Core State Standards, the authors of the standards developed ancillary documents to accompany the standards.

The Common Core State Standards for English Language Arts and Literacy comes with its own set of built-in resources. The appendices of the Common Core are supplemental materials intended to support the implementation of the standards.

- Appendix A includes research and information on how to determine text complexity, recognize text types, and prioritize text types by grade; an explanation of the hybrid approach to grammar and conventions; a chart on the progression of language skills development; strategies for vocabulary development; a bibliography arranged by strands; and a glossary of key terms used in the Common Core Standards document.

- Appendix B contains text exemplars illustrating the complexity, quality, and range of reading appropriate for various grade levels with accompanying sample performance tasks.

- Appendix C includes authentic student writing samples with annotations to illustrate the criteria required to meet the Common Core Standards for writing arguments, information/explanatory text, and narratives in grades K–12.

Pace and Terrell (2011) caution us not to attempt too many new forms of online professional development (PD) at once. We may feel overwhelmed and end up with information overload that we have difficulty adapting to our personal and professional needs. (Read the two special features at the end of this chapter where Kyle Pace and Shelly Terrell share their experiences with technology in the classroom.) Figure 7.1 illustrates the many forms of online PD and networking available to date. No doubt, this list will change as new technologies and ideas arise and others become obsolete as they are replaced with more advanced and effective methods and software. Let's take a look at how these resources relate to literacy leadership.

Educational Technology Online. EdTech Leaders Online at http:// edtechleaders.org will help your district build online courses to enhance professional development, create virtual school programs, and grow electronic learning communities. There are panel discussion forums, online workshops and webinars, professional development programs, funding and grants, featured stories and *EdWeek* articles, and videos.

Education Publications. Ed Pubs at http://www.edpubs.gov offers thousands of free U.S. Department of Education publications. Most are available as downloads versus hard copies.

E-mentoring and E-community Models. Online learning communities are springing up to provide support for student success. One such successful online community that is a collaboration among several groups including the New Teacher Center at the University of California, San Cruz, and the National Science Teachers Association links veteran teachers with teachers new to the profession (Dede, 2006). The advantage and disadvantage of these models is that interaction among participants is asynchronous, meaning participants can read others' responses and post their own at irregular intervals, not at predetermined times. This is advantageous because you can post at your convenience; however, it can be a disadvantage when you need an answer to a problem or issue from your mentor but have to wait for him or her to respond. You can see the potential concern.

Federal Government Resources. Free Federal Resources for Educational Excellence at http://www.free.ed.gov/subjects.cfm?subject_id=78 contains agency resources such as links to sites like Improving Adolescent Literacy: Effective Classroom and Intervention Practices and Integrating Mathematics, Science, and Language. Videos, slideshows, and tools for teaching reading and writing are included.

Literacy Coaching Clearinghouse (LCC). Located at http://ncte.connected community.org/lcc/LCC/Home/, LCC is a connected community of registered members sponsored by the National Council of Teachers of English. The LCC offers resources, blogs, networking opportunities, and a forum to post announcements and events.

Online Webinars. Webinars are Web-based workshops or seminars that provide venues for cyberinteraction among presenters and participants. They are offered online and require participants to register and log into a particular website at a prescribed time to hear and see the scheduled agenda. Just this past month, between the two authors, we attended four online webinars on various topics related to literacy leadership. While one webinar had a low registration fee, the others were offered free of charge. All of the webinars brought in presenters who were well-known experts in their fields, were attended by hundreds of educators across the nation, and could be attended by our colleagues under our—one registrant's—paid registration. We were encouraged by those managing the webinars to share our username and password with colleagues so they could attend at no additional charge. Furthermore, we were e-mailed links to archived presentations after the webinars were over for continued use. We were invited to pass these on to nonregistered colleagues also. These online webinars allowed participants to chat online throughout the conference, post questions and receive answers from the speakers and chat-room monitors, and listen to the speakers while viewing their PowerPoint slides and/or the speakers themselves during their "live" presentations. All four webinars presented up-to-date and cutting-edge information. Some of the perspectives had not yet been published: several speakers mentioned they had publications forthcoming. Webinars offer opportunities for the expedited dissemination of information that exceed the time constraints of traditionally published resources. The following links lead to websites and organizations that offer free and for-a-fee literacy webinars:

- ASCD: Professional Development Webinars at http://www.ascd.org/professional-development/webinars.aspx
- Classroom 2.0 LIVE at http://live.classroom20.com
- Early Literacy Webinars cosponsored by the National Center for Learning Disabilities and the Stern Center for Language and Learning at http://www.getreadytoread.org/index.php?option=com_content&task=view&id=310
- Education Week On-Demand Webinars at http://www.edweek.org/ew/marketplace/webinars/webinars.html#archived
- Global Conversations in Literacy Research at http://globalconversationsinliteracy.wordpress.com/upcoming-webinars
- Literacy, Language, and Leadership: Interested in Learning How to Use Webinars for Literacy PD, Programming, and Promotion? at http://drsaraheaton.wordpress.com/2011/10/05/interested-in-learning-how-to-use-webinars-for-literacy-pd-programming-and-promotion
- Louisiana Department of Education: Webinars and Training Material at http://www.doe.state.la.us/offices/literacy/literacy_webinars_training.html

- Scholastic Read About Webinar Series at http://teacher.scholastic.com/products/ReadAbout/research/webinars.htm
- Teacher-Created Materials Publishing at http://www.teachercreatedmaterials.com/webinars/archive_html
- Triumph Learning: "The Plugged in Webinar Series" at http://www.pluggedintononfiction.com/professional-development/free-webinars
- See also the appendix in this book that provides information on webinars offered by some professional literacy associations.

Public Broadcasting System (PBS). PBS TeacherLine at http://www.pbs.org/teacherline has links to exemplary reading and language arts resources on and outside of the Public Broadcasting System website. You can find effective reading questions that will encourage students to be more engaged readers, as well as videos, lessons, and activities to use in school and with families.

Regional Educational Laboratories (RELs). This network, located at http://ies.ed.gov/ncee/edlabs, consists of 10 laboratories across the United States. They offer access to high-quality, scientifically based education research through technical assistance. The central mission of the RELs is to provide training and disseminate informational resources to state agencies and schools. What does that mean to literacy leaders? If, for example, you want to know what research says about teaching struggling high schoolers to read, or the effectiveness of programs to accelerate vocabulary development in kindergarten, you can search the publications within the REL website for help. If you cannot find a related publication, you can request "Ask A REL" to conduct a search of current research on the topic. You can also sign up for Really Simple Syndication (RSS) feeds that will come right to your desktop. For instance, if you are interested in receiving a copy of an upcoming report on literacy leadership, you can request to receive it as soon as it is available. It will come to your e-mail inbox upon completion.

Social Networks. Twitter, Facebook, Delicious, Flickr, Nings, wikis, and blogs are part of a system of social networks in which the writer can write and "publish" about a topic and readers within an Internet community can choose to respond to share their own thoughts and experiences (Pace & Terrell, 2011). People can start their own blog on a free blog website, such as Livejournal, Wordpress, or Blogger. To "tweet" on Twitter.com or be able to post on the other sites, you log in as a member. Some (e.g., a wiki) can also be used for collaborative projects because they offer all writers the option to edit what has been written by others. Growing in popularity is the http://edcamp.wikispaces.com site—a new type of "education camp" or "unconference." The conference content is driven by which participants choose to sign in. People post workshops they will present at a certain date and time; participants select an agenda based on their interests and professional context and needs. And, they are all free. A literacy leader could arrange an unconference based on the needs of his or her district and invite speakers to present on topics from which teachers could benefit.

On Twitter, there are a number of "hashtags" related to education. By inserting the hashtag symbol (#) in front of a subject, such as #edchat, you can access a network of people talking about a particular topic. Some current subjects are #literacy (literacy chat), #ntchat (new teacher chat), and #reading (reading teachers' chat). You can create your own hashtag conversation without even having a Twitter account. Furthermore, information and news from the U.S. Department of Education will come right to your Twitter account if you become one of usedgov's "followers."

Another type of social network is a "Ning." A couple of Nings that are popular with literacy leaders are the Educator's Personal Learning Network (PLN) and Classroom20.com. The Educator's PLN at http://edupln.ning.com

FIGURE 7.1 The Connected Literacy Leader

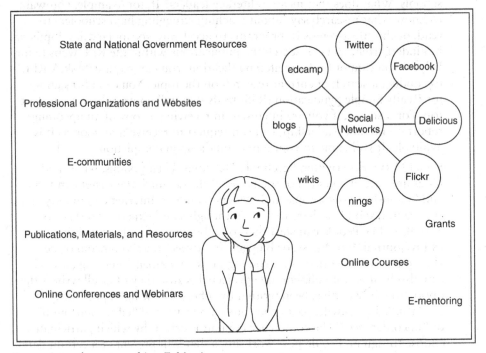

Source: Artwork courtesy of Ann E. Morris.

offers educators forums to chat, videos, blogs, a forum to list upcoming events, and a "leaderboard" that categorizes the most popular posts. Search for terms such as "literacy leaders" or "literacy coaches" to be directed to relevant blogs and resources. Classroom20.com offers links to special-interest groups such as Best Practices for Literacy Instruction, English Language Learners and Literacy, Video Games and Literacy, Professional Development, Distance Collaboration, DigiSkills, Connecting Content and Technology, and many, many others.

While it takes a little time to become familiar and comfortable navigating your way around these networks, the time you invest will be rewarded. Social networks offer readers multiple viewpoints on a topic and a chance to learn from colleagues around the world who are in similar positions (Pace & Terrell, 2011). These sites offer countless connections on the user's time schedule. You may say they represent on-demand professional development and collaboration for prescribed learning (Pace & Terrell, 2011).

Teachers' Domain Professional Development. Teachers' Domain at http://www.teachersdomain.org contains digital media for classrooms and professional development. It offers online courses and teaching strategies by grade and subject.

The Texture of Partnerships

As the opening quote implies, we can all benefit from the support of a knowledgeable, caring "master" to share his or her expertise and experience and lend counsel as we learn. In this part of the chapter, we will look at how mentoring systems and collaborations among groups can grow as purposeful partnerships.

Building Caring Mentorship Relationships

In many states now, schools are required to provide support to new teachers through a mentoring system or program wherein veteran teachers in a district may receive training to effectively guide new teachers through their first year or more of teaching in a district (e.g., see North Carolina's handbook for teacher mentoring at http://www.dpi.state.nc.us/docs/recruitment/beginning/mentorteachershandbook.pdf.) These mentors take the role of literacy leaders when they work with colleagues to shape instruction and curriculum related to reading, writing, listening, speaking, and viewing skills.

Mentoring must be embedded into the culture of a school if it is going to serve its purpose over time (Portner, 2005). Through well-managed, caring mentorship relationships that focus on the development of literacy knowledge and skills, effective practices, motivation to improve as a leader, and professional growth, we are perhaps the best resources available to each other. If your district does not offer a mentoring program to support literacy learning or is seeking to improve its current system, we recommend these sources:

Emelo, R. (2010, March). Building trust-based mentoring relationships. Retrieved from http://www.3creek.com/index.php?/Newsletters/building-trust-based-mentoring-relationships.html. This article describes how to build a trusting, caring mentoring relationship.

Choice Literacy at http://www.choiceliteracy.com. This website's link to Mentoring New Teachers provides featured articles and videos that will help literacy leaders etch out a literacy-mentoring program.

Porter, H. (2005). *Teacher mentoring and induction: The state of the art and beyond.* Thousand Oaks, CA: Corwin Press.

Radford, C. P. (2005). *Mentoring in action: A month-by-month curriculum for mentors and their new teachers.* New York: Allyn & Bacon.

Radford, C. P. (2008). *The first year matters: Being mentored . . . in action.* New York: Allyn & Bacon.

Building Collaborative PD Models

Combining resources within a community can lead to highly effective PD that engages teachers in professional conversations. Many school districts choose to work with local colleges or universities that offer teacher education programs in school-university partnerships. These relationships can benefit both partners as well as students in the K–12 classrooms. Schools we have worked with in school-university partnerships have collaborated to build informed teaching through inquiry, collaborative study of current research, and reflection (Lassonde & Israel, 2010).

Collaboration can also occur among schools and associations. In a recent article in the International Reading Association's *Reading Today* (Scullen, 2010), the author shares the successful combined efforts of the Minnesota Reading Association, the Minnesota Department of Education, and the Minnesota Center for Reading Research to design an annual, three-day PD program called the Leadership in Reading Network (LiRN). Teams of literacy leaders of all kinds—coaches, reading specialists, classroom teachers, administrators, and curriculum professionals—come together to partake in theory-into-practice learning and leave the conference equipped with a newly derived plan for how their team will incorporate what they have learned from the conference into practice and the curriculum. The symbiotic relationship creates "an environment of support and clarity that didn't exist before LiRN was established" (p. 5).

Think of the possibilities available when we venture to reach out and collaborate with others. For example, consider how your district might work with local nonprofit organizations, community groups, or businesses to set up apprenticeship models for authentic and experiential learning. The opportunities are limited only by our imagination, creativity, and willingness to collaborate with stakeholders. Read this chapter's Critical Voices feature in which Shelly shares her ideas and experiences working with stakeholders to integrate technology in her classroom.

Next, we invite you to hear the voices of literacy leaders in the field as you read and contemplate The Ethical Literacy Leader and Critical Voices features in this chapter. Following each feature are questions in the Cultivate Your Leadership Skills section to prompt your thinking as you work toward texturing with resources in your context. To read more about the contributors' backgrounds, see the About the Contributors section.

The Ethical Literacy Leader
Travelling the Narrow Path
—KYLE PACE

Kyle Pace is a K–12 instructional technology specialist and Google-certified teacher from Kansas City, Missouri.

As a K–12 instructional technology specialist, the teachers I work with often say to me, "I am just so afraid to have my students use _____ in the classroom." Fill in that blank with any popular search engine or Web-based tool that's popular today. You get the idea. Or maybe you've heard this one, too: "My district blocks _____ because there's too much bad stuff out there." Again, fill in that blank appropriately.

If we want to be schools that are really stepping out there to create new, real learning opportunities for our students, then we can't let fear of what's out there forever cast the bigger shadow. At the same time, it's always easier to travel that "wider path" that the majority of our schools are on. Just blocking this, banning that, you know the routine. Is there digital junk out there? Absolutely there is. Are there inappropriate digital places we need to protect our students from? Most definitely. But guess what? This isn't a secret to our students.

Connect, Collect, Curate, Create

Teachers and students alike now have access to unlimited amounts of learning via the Internet. It has forever changed how we learn. We want our students to be able to use these sites, tools, and online spaces to maximize their learning experiences and see that the Web doesn't have to be a scary place. However, we (parents, teachers, teacher leaders) must make this a learning priority for ourselves first. We must be willing to travel the narrow path. Along that path come a time commitment, refinement, and reflection on what works and what doesn't work.

Getting *connected* in online spaces offers teachers and students alike new ways to learn. Developing a personal learning network (PLN) can become as reliable, if not more reliable, than going to a search engine to seek out new information and ideas. This might be following blogs, joining Twitter, building circles on Google+, or joining a Ning network. Whatever the medium, getting connected in digital spaces with like-minded educators can be a very rewarding learning experience.

After getting connected and fostering your network for a while, we begin to *collect* from our network. Resources and ideas begin to abound. We need to model how to effectively collect these resources as they come in. This might be using Google Reader for the different blogs you want to follow, or checking out a specific hashtag on Twitter. It might also mean exploring the uses of Google Docs or Evernote to collect all the great stuff coming in from your network.

Just like the person in charge of getting all the best exhibits and artifacts for a museum, it is important to be able to properly *curate* all of these collected items. Discover which ones are the best, and get them organized in a way that you can quickly access them again later when you need them for a particular lesson or project in class. These can be published via a wiki or Google site, or tools like Diigo and Delicious come in very handy to curate the best of the best that your online network PD has provided.

Then ultimately, after we have become connected and we begin collecting information and ideas and curating the very best ones, we have ourselves prepped and ready to *create* new instructional content for our students. Students need to be creating also. We cannot expect our students to consume, consume, consume all day long. Students do enough

consumption from the Internet on their own. The learning experience should include students creating high-quality content that not only demonstrates their learning, but also, when they share it back with their network or publish it to their site, blog, YouTube channel, and so forth, can possibly be of benefit to students all over the world.

I believe that Howard Rheingold (2011) expressed it best when he explained that these should not be treated just as skills, but should be new literacies in education. The information is there, and we as teachers first need to know how to get the really best stuff from these digital spaces, so we can teach our students how to effectively do the same. These skills (literacies) will last a lifetime, no matter what career path our students choose. We must be willing to take the narrow path and hold the course. The wide path has been around forever and it's very over-traveled.

Cultivate Your Leadership Skills

1. What do you think Kyle means by "The wide path has been around forever and it's very over-traveled"? Does this statement reflect the perceptions in your school?
2. What is your personal comfort level with technology? How does it influence your role as a literacy leader?
3. How do you and your school connect, collect, curate, and create?

Critical Voices
Collaborating with Stakeholders
—SHELLY TERRELL

Shelly Terrell is a teacher trainer, international speaker, and author. Her prolific presence in the educator community through social media has been recognized.

Literacy leaders play a difficult role when carrying out an action plan and ensuring all stakeholders feel they have a voice that influences the implementation of that action plan. Teachers, parents, and students will have strong opinions and beliefs about what is needed and what is appropriate in the school community.

As a teacher, I have always been very eager to test new ground, especially when it comes to integrating technology into the curriculum. However, throughout the more than 15 years I have used technology in the classroom, I have met with many parents, administrators, and students who resisted the technology.

One of the earliest technologies I integrated into the classroom was using a tape recorder to record my students' dialogues. Parents were not happy about having their children recorded. Much later, when I began teaching in Germany, I wanted to publish my preschoolers' drawings and voices online for a global digital storytelling project. Having remembered the resistance to the technology in the past, I decided to host an education technology workshop for parents where I could show them what I planned to do and get their permission.

I started by asking them what they felt about technology. One parent raised his hand and told me he felt that technology made this generation of children lazy and stupid. Many of the parents nodded their heads in agreement. I was shocked by such a bold statement but knew I had to persuade the parents of the benefits of using technology. I began to show the parents examples of English-language

learners who were my students' ages who had published work online. The parents were amazed at the learning and creativity. This helped them and even my director get excited about the use of technology in the classroom. We compromised and came to agreements about the use that made both sides comfortable. One agreement was that I would not post photographs of their children online. Instead, I used avatars or cartoonlike faces to represent the children.

Literacy leadership should certainly allow some of the opinions and beliefs of stakeholders to influence certain changes. However, certain issues arise, such as: how much change should be allowed that does not compromise the original mission statement of the school; and how does literacy leadership ensure stakeholders feel they have been listened to, even when certain changes are not made?

I have worked with literacy leadership that handles these issues in various ways. One leader I worked with decided to cut off the communication and discourse. When a decision was made about the integration of technology, it could not be questioned. This leader hid in the office and would not take any questions or respond to any disagreeing thoughts from teachers or students. The stakeholders felt ignored.

In another case, I have seen literacy leadership that is too flexible to the point I felt the leader was bullied and many didn't respect that leader. Great literacy leaders realize disagreement and discourse are part of the process, especially when it comes to introducing new, progressive ideas and approaches. Effective leaders design strategies for handling this. However, great literacy leaders also cultivate relationships in the beginning and ensure stakeholders realize they do have influence and a voice.

Great literacy leaders promote effective communication even when communication is uncomfortable. As a teacher I would love to be able to use technology in many ways, but I have learned to compromise and work with parents and administrators. I find their support—achieved through communication and sometimes compromise—makes the technology integration much easier.

Cultivate Your Leadership Skills

1. How might Shelly have partnered or collaborated with stakeholders to advance her students' literacy and technology knowledge and use?
2. Shelly says, "As a teacher I would love to be able to use technology in many ways, but I have learned to compromise and work with parents and administrators." What does this statement imply about how Shelly views compromise?
3. Review the list of online professional development options described in this chapter. Which, if any, do you think the administrators or parents might be cautious of you using with the students in your district?

Closing Thoughts

"The guidance of a master" to which Cennini refers in the quote at the beginning of this chapter can take on many different forms, as we've noted in this chapter. From professional associations and the journals, white papers, and position papers they produce, to online PD and the networking opportunities it offers, there are a wide selection and variety of "masters" from whom to learn. We suggest you experiment with resources outside of your comfort zone. You may be surprised at how navigable, beneficial, and enjoyable they are!

Questions for Reflection and Discussion

1. Which resources in this chapter were new to you? Which ones have you tried and liked? Which ones have you tried but not liked?

2. What determines whether a resource is helpful or not to you?

3. What other resources would you include?

4. Do you believe there is such a thing as being "too networked"? What might this look like? What might be the results?

5. How do we assess the effectiveness of online PD? Do our school district administrators value it as much as on- or off-site PD? What other issues does online PD spark?

6. Reflect on what it would take to make you feel comfortable using a resource or participating in a group you have never previously tried.

7. Coming full circle, reread Cennini's quote at the beginning of this chapter. Now that you've read and reflected on this chapter, what or whom do you see as more or less valuable "masters" to whom you would feel comfortable reaching out and learning from?

Practical Applications

How might this chapter apply to your teaching context and experience? Try these activities:

Classroom Activity

Select one or two resources from this chapter to try out in your classroom. Ask your students to provide feedback for you.

Professional Development Activity

With a group of colleagues, split up the list of resources included in this chapter. Each member of the group can explore several resources and report back to the larger group. Share your thoughts about the resources. Were they practical? Could they be helpful to certain students or colleagues in your district? How might they be helpful?

Also, collaborate to create a listing of additional resources that you know about and research to add to the listing in this chapter. The listing could be shared electronically or in hard copy with all teachers as a way to model a transformative literacy-community accomplishment. Invite everyone to add their favorite resources to the list for all to share.

References

Dede, C. (Ed.). (2006). *Online professional development for teachers: Emerging models and methods.* Cambridge, MA: Harvard Education Press.

Lassonde, C., & Israel, S. E. (2010). *Teacher collaboration for professional learning: Facilitating study, research, and inquiry communities.* San Francisco, CA: Jossey-Bass.

Pace, K., & Terrell, S. (2011, October). Tapping the power of online professional development. A webinar sponsored by Global Scholar and *Education Week* at http://www.edweek.org/go/webinar.

Portner, H. (2005). Embedding induction and mentoring into a school's culture. In H. Partner, (Ed.), *Teacher mentoring and induction: The state of the art and beyond* (pp. 75–94). Thousand Oaks, CA: Corwin Press.

Rheingold, H. (Producer). (2011, February 17). *Crap detection 101* [Video]. Retrieved from http://www.youtube.com/watch?v=AHVvGELuEqM

Scullen, J. (2011, October/November). Minnesota Reading Association partners with State DOE to provide professional development for literacy leaders of all kinds. *Reading Today, 29*(2), 4–5.

Wright, J. (2007). *The RTI toolkit: A practical guide for schools.* Port Chester, NY: National Professional Resources, Inc.

Celebrating the Masterpiece

> ❝Finally, good painting is a music and a melody which intellect only can appreciate, and with great difficulty. ❞
>
> —MICHELANGELO

> ❝Once you have tasted flight, you will walk the earth with your eyes turned skywards, for there you have been and there you will long to return. ❞
>
> —LEONARDO DA VINCI

We come to the final chapter. In our efforts to inspire you as you close this book on literacy leadership and move forward to apply it to your part of the world, we actually begin our last chapter with two quotes. We found these quotes about how Michelangelo and da Vinci describe their art and talent both so inspiring we couldn't leave either out. We hope you connect with them as well.

If Michelangelo and da Vinci were alive today, they might certainly agree that, as a nation, we must invest in our students' literacy development in the same way that those who appreciate and value good art invest thousands in beautiful paintings. Our children are our masterpieces, our "music and melody" and our "flight," as Michelangelo and da Vinci would say. These metaphors can also be applied to the beautiful literacy community you have begun to create and will continue to refine as a result, in part, of applying the knowledge and methods you've learned in this book.

In this, our final chapter, we look at assessing the progress of our literacy communities and students' progress as a result of the effectiveness of our literacy programs. As we stand back and look at our masterpiece, what do we see? Are we satisfied with what we've achieved and how we've done it? Where is there room for improvement? As you read this chapter, continue to reflect on how you can help your school create a community of masterful paintings.

Assessing Progress

At the time of the writing of this book, there is much talk about the imminent introduction of progressive models of teacher evaluation based on the value-added component of matching teacher pay to student performance, even though lack of funding causes schools to cut teaching positions and programs that support instruction. Educators struggle with how to interpret and implement new standards and policies. And, debates still rage over the effects and purpose of high-stakes testing in schools, even while the Partnership for Assessment of Readiness for College and Careers (PARCC) is building K–12 assessments in English and math. Assessment and evaluation can be perceived as misguided and perhaps threatening to some. However, when we look at assessment as a way to inform, improve, and increase one's knowledge, skills, and dispositions, it becomes a way to invest in our masterpiece.

To determine the effectiveness, strengths, and weaknesses of a school's literacy leadership, the program's, teachers', and students' progress must be continually assessed through multiple measures. No one test on its own, standing alone, should be used as a measure. It would be wrong to judge the effectiveness of one's efforts, for example, by just comparing students' annual yearly progress in reading and the language arts.

The question in assessing progress in literacy leadership becomes not *should* we assess, but *how* and *what* do we assess? How do we know whether or not our efforts are contributing to transformation and progress in our literacy program? Throughout this book, we have strongly supported collaborative, team leadership; proactive communication; and experiential education. Rather than prescribe one method for assessing progress, we encourage schools to enact the principles put forth in this book to compose custom-made methods for assessing the effectiveness of the literacy leadership in their schools.

Collaborative, Team Leadership

Using the principle of collaborative, team leadership to track and evaluate the effectiveness of its literacy program and leadership efforts, the school's literacy-learning community should determine what it values in students' literacy development and in instructional teaching methods. No doubt, continuous and careful monitoring of a literacy program is an integral approach to determining the most successful methods, approaches, and strategies for teaching reading and writing. It helps teachers identify and teach to affect student achievement. Therefore, careful monitoring and evaluating reveal the effectiveness of the team's leadership.

The literacy-learning community should discuss and decide on

- its purpose for evaluating,
- what it needs to evaluate,
- when to evaluate,
- how it will evaluate and monitor, and, in retrospect,
- how well it has evaluated.

Translating Values into Action

The key is to monitor and evaluate the effectiveness of a literacy community on a regular basis. Some may be unsure how to do this, and therefore be so overwhelmed with determining how and where to begin that they fail to determine a focus to design a manageable and useful monitoring process. We recommend starting by assessing one or two needs, then setting goals for how to evaluate them. For example, a district's needs might include

- building a knowledge base about literacy;
- structuring curriculum to meet the Common Core State Standards (see Tracey Johnson's The Common Core State Standards Connection feature in this chapter); and
- identifying environmental factors that may affect student reading achievement.

Goals might include

- forming study groups to review current literacy research;
- formulating focus questions to design the evaluation process; and
- developing monitoring techniques to evaluate the effectiveness of literacy coaching on student achievement.

Resetting Goals

Once goals are achieved, the cycle begins again. Needs are assessed, goals are formed, and progress is monitored and evaluated. The work of the collaborative leadership community is flexible and ongoing, evolving with the values and needs of the community and students. Before moving on to new goals, however, we recommend celebrating your achievements.

The Common Core State Standards Connection

Continue to Press Toward the Mark

TRACEY JOHNSON

Tracey's career in education spans over 22 years. She has taught at all educational levels, developed curriculum, provided professional development to persistently low-achieving schools, and mentored teachers.

The Common Core State Standards initiative has made its mark in the educational history of America. The overarching goal or "mark" is to ensure that no matter where students live, they are prepared for success in postsecondary education and the workforce. This huge undertaking has spurred a need to collaborate across states, legislative agencies, and educational institutions to develop instructional materials and resources, provide professional development, and create assessments to ensure that the standards are implemented successfully.

It is imperative that educators and local and state policymakers work in tandem to align their goals on key areas that require attention and work, as states transition to the standards. Although school districts are faced with dire fiscal constraints, and sometimes opposing societal issues, highly effective instructional programs and learning opportunities must not be compromised or go uncelebrated. Education agencies and institutions will have to keep their focus and press toward the mark, which is to provide students of the 21st century an education to ensure that they will be successful citizens who are college and career ready. And, isn't that reason to celebrate?

Celebrating Successes

"Everyone's coming over to my house tonight to celebrate Marta. Can you come? Nothing fancy. Just some pizza."

"Sounds like fun. Is it Marta's birthday?"

"No, she was just awarded a grant so she could go to International Reading Association in Chicago! She's going to do a workshop on the writing strategies she uses with her students. She just found out today, so we're throwing an impromptu pizza party to celebrate."

Whether you celebrate successes by joining together to support a colleague's achievements, accomplishments, or efforts, or by putting your feet up at the end of a long day to reflect on the success a struggling reader in your class had with a new approach you used to teach phonics, celebrations acknowledge, reward, and commemorate our literacy work. How are literacy leaders celebrating successes in big and small ways?

Sometimes we are recognized for our efforts and celebrate through recognition. Here's an example. The Learning Alliance of Indian River County in East Vero Beach, Florida, is a nonprofit organization that was founded by a group of concerned parents who saw their children struggling and failing with traditional educational methods. Large numbers of students were failing the reading portion of the Florida Comprehensive Assessment Test. The Learning Alliance has as its goal to radically improve the literacy rates of children with the help of partnerships between civic youth organizations, universities, philanthropists, schools, nonprofit organizations, and parents. Recently, the Learning Alliance awarded all 13 elementary school principals with plaques—tipping their hat to the schools' staff, parents, and the community as well—to commemorate the schools' success in markedly improving student literacy over the past year. The Florida State Department of Education further recognized nine of these schools by rating them with a grade of "A" and the remaining four schools with a grade of "B."

Other times we celebrate with our students by organizing special events. Schools hold community celebrations to share students' work such as Authors Nights, Celebrity Read-Alouds, and Book Fairs. Read Dawn Hamlin's Response to Intervention (RTI) and the Literacy Leader feature in this chapter for suggestions for celebrating with students.

And, still other times we celebrate with a personal sigh of relief. Celebrations—whether they are big or small, public or private, personal or shared—are important. They provide the closure we need to fortify us so we have the strength to move on to confront and tackle upcoming challenges. Celebrate the little things. Celebrate the big achievements. Celebrate the everyday good you do. Read Janet Richards's The Ethical Literacy Leader feature in this chapter to see how she celebrates with students and colleagues.

Response to Intervention (RTI) and the Literacy Leader

Celebrating Achievements

—DAWN HAMLIN

Dawn is a former special education teacher who taught in both traditional public schools and residential facilities. She currently is assistant professor at SUNY College at Oneonta, where she helped develop the graduate program in special education. She is also past president of the New York State Council for Exceptional Children.

One of the best things about the data collection process of RTI has to be the graphs. It constantly amazes me how many students are fascinated and intrinsically motivated by results on their data graphs. For many it appears to be easier to see their improvement via a graph than to compare other forms of their work. Often I will have the students graph with me and we will compare. Did our numbers match? How long did it take us to reach our personal goal? A critical component of all of these graphs is the goal line. When we initially set up a graph with a student, we will carefully pick a quickly and easily attainable short-term goal. This will provide students with access to quick gratification and a sense of achievement. In turn, their motivation to reach the next goal typically increases. Just knowing that they have already been successful gives them confidence to go for that next "brass ring."

Sometimes students are motivated to celebrate achievements with simple extrinsic rewards. When a student reaches his or her goal, I am ready to celebrate with some reward that is meaningful for that individual student. For some it may be a special sticker or pencil. For others it may be a public announcement or their name on an all-star board. For some it may be five minutes of free time with a favorite computer game or playing a game

with a friend, as long as it is meaningful to that particular child. That is the key to effective rewards. The main idea, however, is to celebrate—and celebrate often and in varying ways. (For ideas on rewards, look at the Behavior Interventions reinforcer menu at http://www.interventioncentral.org.)

One part that plays a very important role in our celebrations is a discussion on what went well and why exactly the student succeeded. This may also include the student reviewing his or her work and helping—with guidance—to choose a new goal. This child-centered goal setting develops the beginning of self-regulation—an important strategy for future success.

Don't forget to celebrate with your colleagues as well—perhaps when a certain student hits a particular milestone or a targeted group of students all pass a high-stakes test. Take the time to reward yourselves! Have a teachers-go-to-the-movies night or maybe a special breakfast before the day starts. Even "woo-hoo" cards will make people feel appreciated and help to build a positive, successful team. In an era when many educators feel under the gun and overwhelmed, it is imperative to take the time to enjoy success and keep up your enthusiasm!

Redefining Our Role and Job Description

As educators and literacy leaders, we cannot control all of the changes that evolve in our school, government, and society. Change is inevitable for various reasons: economic, political, and professional. We can be proactive and voice our opinions. We can act boldly. But we cannot stop or even always control change.

This book calls out to educators to be agents of change themselves. It shouts, "Become a literacy leader!" By this we mean: Rethink what your current role is and how you perceive your position in the community and school. Turn your attention to think and act in ways that promote mentorship, authentic engagement in and belonging fully to a literacy-learning community. Use the principles set forth in this book to change the current story of literacy education in powerful ways.

Closing Thoughts

DuFour, DuFour, and Eaker (2008) tell us the recognition of people and their victories is the best way to sustain momentum for change. Making victories visible gives people the nudge and the courage to say, "If they can do it, so can I." Kegan and Lahey (2001) state that feeling valued by others because of the work we do is one of our "deepest hungers" (p. 92). We all want to be recognized for our efforts. It makes us feel appreciated. That's why we have Mother's Day and Father's Day. Right? Our efforts might go unnoticed every other day, but on Mother's Day, isn't it great to hear someone say, "Thanks for all you do"?

Appreciation and recognition aren't the only reasons for celebration, though. Reflect back to the anecdote Kristine shared about reading with her son Mathew in Chapter 1. We saw how Mathew and Kristine were both literacy leaders, not because they had a job description that said they were, but because they took a certain path. The path they took will lead them to new adventures and new worlds. It will transform them. This is reason to celebrate.

We've come to the end of the chapter and the end of the book. We hope you will walk away with new understandings, strengthened commitment, and a new sense of confidence to inspire your work with children and adults.

Yours is an important role in our education system. We respect and honor your contributions to the field of literacy, and we're elated that if in some small way we have helped you move further along your chosen path as a literacy leader. We appreciate and recognize your efforts and your work. We celebrate YOU!

Now is the time to embrace the possibilities that will transform literacy education, learning, and schooling. We have the knowledge and resources we need to restore balance to our wounded schools. We just need to know how to disseminate and apply it. Through effective literacy leadership in our schools and communities, we can evoke the spirit, soul, and intellect we need to design, construct, and celebrate our masterpiece of literacy-learning communities.

One final time, we invite you to hear the voices of literacy leaders in the field as you read and contemplate The Ethical Literacy Leader and Critical Voices features in this chapter. Following each feature are questions in the Cultivate Your Leadership Skills section to prompt your thinking as you work toward celebrating the masterpiece of literacy leadership in your context. To read more about all of our contributors' backgrounds, see the About the Contributors section of this book.

The Ethical Literacy Leader
Celebrating Successes Through "Star Tattoos"
—JANET RICHARDS

Janet, professor of literacy and research at the University of South Florida, supervises field-based courses at a local community center, where she mentors her graduate students in a Community of Practice model. In this caring structure, doctoral and master's students learn to become literacy leaders.

Everyone likes a pat on the back for good work. For example, just last week I modeled a writing strategy with a small group of second-grade children as some teachers in a literacy-leader cohort observed. One little girl, Sarah, in the writing group tried her best to engage with me in the strategy while the other three children, for reasons unknown, tried their best to disengage from the group. At the end of the session, I complimented Sarah and asked if she would like a "star tattoo" on her hand to remind her of her exceptional work. She readily agreed that the tattoo I created with a pink, fine-line marker was just what she wanted. The other three children looked enviously at Sarah's

reward as I commented, "Everyone deserves a star tattoo to celebrate their success and accomplishments."

This small teaching moment was a major learning point for the teachers in the literacy-leader cohort. No, I don't mean they learned to actually place star tattoos on exceptional reading and writing teachers' hands. But they did immediately recognize the importance of placing metaphorical star tattoos on all teachers' hands.

Following Sarah's star tattoo celebration, I seized the teaching moment and built on her success by asking the literacy leaders to consider how Sarah's star moment might connect to their future work with teachers. Here are two general, paraphrased questions that arose from our conversation.

> Sarah was thrilled, but what about the other three children? Might they feel so envious they'll never believe in themselves?
> How can I as a literacy leader celebrate a teacher's pedagogical success when I know a celebration will probably lead to other teachers' envy and resentment?

Here is one of my responses to these astute questions.

> We've all learned in our preservice teacher days to catch a child being good. Literacy leaders who remember and follow that metaphor always look for the good—not the bad—and they build on those small teacher moments of success.

The group of future literacy leaders immediately got the message. Typical responses included comments like (paraphrased) the following:

> We don't have to wait for *big* accomplishments to have a celebration.
> We can celebrate the small moments of teachers' successes.
> When we celebrate small moments, every teacher receives accolades.

My second response to the group focused on what to do when a teacher receives a *big* celebration for an accomplishment.

> There is no doubt a teacher's *big* accomplishment certainly deserves a celebration. However, at the same time, effective literacy leaders can reward all teachers who work toward a common goal,

who have achieved their stated objectives for literacy teaching and learning, and who have served as inspiration to others. In other words, effective literacy leaders work to gradually alter the school culture so all teachers are helpmates and can share in their own and peers' successes.

This sharp group of future literacy leaders got the gist of this message also. Representative responses included comments like (paraphrased) the following:

> We might have end-of-year celebrations for all.
> I could write monthly notes of appreciation to all teachers.
> I could have teachers collaborate in teams.
> We could celebrate the shared knowledge of teachers.

The comments of these future literacy leaders portray their visionary thinking about celebrating successes. They know it is important to celebrate small successes and *big* accomplishments. They recognize the benefits of collaboration. Equally important, they understand how to "catch" all teachers' achievements and celebrate their star tattoo successes often.

Cultivate Your Leadership Skills

1. How does Janet's star tattoo experience connect with the ideas presented in this chapter?
2. Reflecting on Michelangelo's and da Vinci's quotes at the beginning of this chapter, what do the star tattoos represent?
3. How does Janet's experience fit with the ways your school assesses literacy programs, progress, and learning?

Critical Voices

Supporting Literacy Leadership

—KRISLYNN DENGLER

Krislynn has served as a high school principal at a rural, upstate New York public school. She currently serves as chair-elect for the Reading and English Language Arts Special Interest Group for the Association of Teacher Educators and teaches methods-level courses to preservice teachers.

I was fortunate to be one of many literacy leaders at the high school where I was principal. Early in my tenure, I remember worrying about being the kind of leader who could instigate change, but not leave roots enough for it to be sustainable when there were inevitable changes in administration. I can proudly say I led by example and encouraged and supported others to access their natural abilities to be literacy leaders.

Prior to the budget cuts, there were formative years where teachers were talking about students needing more critical reading skills as well as having an overall need in the area of writing. Those memories are linked to some exciting times as these educators became literacy leaders in their own right, some with more hesitation than others, but most of us were on the same path.

One leader worked to offer students a course to help them read better and gain information from textbooks; another to get reluctant readers to read small (read "doable"), exciting novels in a strategic reading (non-English) class; a duo breathed life into the forensics program and increased student membership (as well as community recognition); one added a challenging classic novel to her elective science class (she also organized and empowered students to exhibit and present their best academic work in an all-school, all-subject academic fair that teachers, parents, friends, relatives, community members, and board of education members attended). Another encouraged and supported students to

re-create the student newspaper (online version), giving an opportunity for voice that had been shelved for quite some time; yet another sat with a small group of students who had yet to find their fit in the "regular" school structure, and worked with these readers and writers to become just that. Five teachers joined me to create a professional learning community of teachers as professional education readers (TAPER) (Allington, 2012) to take the opportunity to critically read and reflect on new ideas in teaching and learning with the goal of sharing innovative concepts with our colleagues.

Fast forward to the budget woes...

Rumors began early about drastic cuts being made in the upcoming budget season. Nerves began to fray as the first budget draft became public. The proposal and eventuality included the scrapping of many of the efforts previously mentioned through course reductions, and restructuring some and deleting other programs and clubs—all under the semblance of saving money.

In response, a representative group of high school seniors sought my advice and support in addressing the board of education about their concerns regarding what was being proposed. The students constructed a 15-minute (or more) treatise on all of the benefits they had been fortunate enough to gain through their years in high school. They named names and referred to specific events and opportunities afforded to them, pleading with the board of education and school superintendent to find alternative ways to make the needed financial adjustments; to not diminish the prospects for their sisters, brothers, cousins, friends, peers.

The result included some literacy leaders being cut, several vacancies through attrition being unfilled, some leaders being reassigned to include travelling during their day between the middle and high schools, and the middle school reading program being eliminated altogether. Worst of all, that small program for those students who had truly just begun to believe they could be readers and writers was discarded, forcing them to make choices about whether or not to rejoin the system that had failed them.

Did our superintendent and board of education really think they were making choices in the best interest of our current and future literacy leaders and learners? I suppose not, but I do presume when they looked at the alternative cost, they hedged their bet. At last check, two years gone by, not much has changed in the decision making of that school, yet our literacy leaders continue to lead on in very meaningful ways (to their credit).

Despite the tremendous shift in the teaching load expectation, the new Race to the Top initiative, and continued budget woes, some of our best and brightest find ways to continue to quietly (in most cases) lead. For example, a pair of literacy leaders continues to offer their own time and support to review oral recitations for students who prepare narrations like *Potter's Field* for community events such as Memorial Day celebrations. Another leader, after taking a break, is once again organizing and lobbying students to participate in exhibiting their accomplishments at the high school academic fair. A handful of others create extra-help time with students in their aim for understanding.

Cultivate Your Leadership Skills

1. How are you a literacy leader?
2. How can you promote literacy leadership in your students? Peers?
3. Do changes and restructuring sometimes dissuade literacy leaders from leading? What does this do to student morale?

Questions for Reflection and Discussion

1. Write a job description for your current or target position in education. How might that description express your role as a literacy leader to complement whatever position you hold?

2. How does your school assess and monitor the progress and effectiveness of your literacy-leadership community?

3. In what ways do you celebrate the masterpieces of literacy leadership and students' literacy progress in your school? Do your celebrations affect your personal or your school's progress, effectiveness, or efforts?

4. After reading this chapter, what new ways could you create to celebrate the little and big leadership successes in your school?

5. Coming full circle, reread Michelangelo's and da Vinci's quotes that begin this chapter. Now that you've read and reflected on this chapter, how do you see their words reflected in the arena of celebrating the masterpiece of literacy leadership?

Practical Applications

How might this chapter apply to your teaching context and experience? Try these activities:

Classroom Activity

Take the opportunity to celebrate students as literacy leaders in your classroom. Observe and note which students act as models for others in their passion to read and write and to support the literacy growth of others. How might you recognize their leadership and encourage others to become literacy leaders also?

Professional Development Activity

This chapter asks us to "Turn your attention to think and act in ways that promote mentorship, authentic engagement in and belonging fully to a literacy-learning community." What might this look like in your school?

Talk with colleagues about how you might collaborate to develop or enhance an already existing literacy-learning community. How might you start or inspire an initiative to become more proactive literacy leaders?

References

Allington, R. L. (2012). *What really matters for struggling readers: Designing research-based programs.* Boston: Pearson.

DuFour, R., DuFour, R., & Eaker, R. (2008). *Revisiting professional learning communities at work: New insights for improving schools.* Bloomington, IN: Solution Tree Press.

Kegan, R., & Lahey, L. (2001). *How the way we talk can change the way we work: Seven languages for transformation.* San Francisco: Jossey-Bass.

Appendix

Literacy Professional Associations

American Reading Company

Jane Hileman, CEO and Founder American Reading Company (ARC) partners with school districts to create a Common Core State Standards–based ecosystem, bias-free learning environments, and whole–school turnarounds. Through elbow-to-elbow executive coaching, ARC helps principals and district administrators reorganize their schools around continuous improvement using accountability systems that track the average rate of reading growth in each classroom. ARC's accountability system is built upon a Common Core State Standards–based assessment system called the Independent Reading Level Assessment (IRLA). The IRLA allows teachers to level books and students, match students to books of appropriate challenge, diagnose individual reading strengths and areas of need, and develop Action Plans for each student. The IRLA, combined with the 100 Book Challenge intensive reading-practice system and the Web-based student and classroom data collection and analysis system, SchoolPace, allows for formative assessment, precision instruction, and careful, daily tracking of student progress. ACTION 100 further infuses these components into a 12-step whole-school reform model providing a multi-tiered support system for students, parents, and educators. ACTION 100 helps schools organize all resources to focus on literacy engagement and dramatic improvements in achievement in reading, science, and social studies.

Resources for Literacy Leaders

Websites

www.americanreading.com provides descriptions of all materials and services offered.

www.americanreadingathome.com offers resources for parents to teach their preschool children to read using ARC materials, coaching tips, and videos.

Professional Development

ARC provides intensive, on-site coaching for leaders and the teachers they supervise, helping them implement ARC programs with fidelity and effectiveness. Professional development modules of 5 to 30 or more days are available and are tailored to fit the needs of the school or district.

Literacy-leadership courses are also offered to administrators, literacy coaches, and model-classroom teachers. These courses combine study of professional literature with hands-on, in-class experiences using ARC's formative assessment tools.

Conferences

ARC hosts regular Colloquia and Symposiums led by members of its Academic Advisory Board (e.g. Richard Allington, Pedro Noguera, Alma Flor Ada, and other nationally known literacy leaders).

Publications

- Action 100 Leadership Framework
- Independent Reading Level Assessment: Common Core State Standards (IRLA-CCSS)
- Instructional Framework (K–1, 2–5, secondary)
- Research Labs: Project-Based Learning Units in Science and Social Studies (thematic units for over 50 topics)
- Zoology One: a full reading, writing, and science unit for beginning readers (late pre-K or kindergarten)
- Reading On-Ramp for new readers, 300 published titles to teach first steps of reading
- Educating Black and Latino Males: Striving for Excellence

Materials

Over 1,000 leveled informational and literary text collections for all grades pre-K through 12, leveled according to Common Core State Standards Text Complexity Strands, for

- wide reading
- genre study
- science themes
- social studies themes

All materials and programs are also available in Spanish.

School Improvement Grants (SIG)

ARC is key partner with several SIG schools and can assist in writing SIG applications.

Technological Resources

SchoolPace: online data collection, analysis, and reporting system that delivers daily updates to literacy leaders showing where their schools and students are in progressing toward achieving specific literacy goals.

IRLA-CCSS Online: allows teachers to record and track individual student progress and plan instruction based on the Common Core State Standards.

Americanreading@home is a parent support website with coaching tips and 300 digital emergent reading books that can be downloaded from Google App and used on any device.

American Reading Forum

Nance Wilson, Chair: Michael French, Chair of Publications Committee

The American Reading Forum is an organization that facilitates the dissemination of ideas and research regarding literacy instruction and the preparation of literacy educators at the graduate and undergraduate levels. At the heart of the organization is its mission for providing members with opportunities for collaboration, discussion, and exploration of emerging research interests and paradigms as related to literacy through a mutual exchange of ideas. The goal of the organization is threefold: (1) to provide opportunities for members to generate new research, share and refine research in progress, report on completed research, and evaluate existing research; (2) to provide for the application of research, theory, and philosophical deliberations into sound practice; and (3) to conduct an annual conference and produce a yearbook in which members can disseminate and discuss new ideas. In addition, through formal mentoring activities, newly trained scholars and scholars in training can get to know and get assistance from established and distinguished scholars in the field.

At the annual conference of the American Reading Forum, members have a unique opportunity to gather and discuss issues of literacy research and instruction in a variety of formats. In addition to the common conference session formats (paper sessions, major addresses, and symposia), the American Reading Forum offers alternative formats to enhance opportunities for participants' interaction. These formats include multiple receptions, problems courts focused on involving all members in discussions of multiple viewpoints, panel sessions to share varied viewpoints, and a Call to Forum during which members discuss a common reading or media source and its implications for and applications to both research and classroom teaching. Throughout the entire conference, newly trained scholars and scholars in training are encouraged to be active participants and to take part in the formal mentoring and research exchange meetings that are annually scheduled.

The American Reading Forum annually publishes a yearbook chronicling the research presented at the conference. The yearbook is peer reviewed and published online to allow for free access to all interested parties.

There are many opportunities for members to become involved in the American Reading Forum. Members are engaged in international projects, mentoring, research exchange, and the development of the annual conference program. In addition, the American Reading Forum maintains an active listserv where members continue the rich conversations of the conference throughout the year.

For more information regarding the American Reading Forum, please visit: http://americanreadingforum.org/index.shtml.

Association of Literacy Educators and Researchers

Mary Roe, Past President; John Smith, President; Rob Erwin, President-Elect The Association of Literacy Educators and Researchers (ALER) prides itself on offering a friendly and supportive professional community. ALER's four goals evidence its attention to teaching and research: (1) to promote standards and competencies within the profession; (2) to stimulate the self-development and professional growth of teachers and reading specialists at all educational levels; (3) to support the continuing improvement of college and university curricula and encourage preparation programs for teachers and reading specialists; and (4) to encourage the continuing improvement of administrative, clinical, diagnostic, and instructional practices related to the learning process. These goals are moved forward collectively and through the four ALER divisions: Adult Learning, Clinical Research and Practice, College Literacy, and Teacher Education. For example, the Adult Learning Division examines issues of instructional practices, family literacy, and workforce education. The Clinical Research and Practice Division supports university reading clinics and tutoring programs, and explores the reading process and its application to clinical, diagnostic, instructional, and administrative elements. The College Literacy Division focuses on literacy practices and methods for teaching postsecondary students at all achievement levels, including development-level reading, writing, study skills, and ESL courses. The Teacher Education Division addresses teacher-education practices at the undergraduate and graduate levels, promoting improvement of preservice and inservice programs for literacy development.

ALER sponsors an annual conference at various locations within the United States. Attendees can choose from a range of topics offered by the presenters as well as the invited keynote speakers. ALER publishes the peer-reviewed journal *Literacy Research and Instruction*, a peer-reviewed ALER yearbook featuring conference presentations, and commissioned white papers. To acknowledge professional accomplishments, ALER annually honors various award recipients. The J. Estill Alexander Future Leaders in Literacy award identifies outstanding master's and doctoral students' research. The A. B. Herr award recognizes a professional educator who has made outstanding contributions to the field of reading, while a more junior but accomplished scholar receives the Jerry Johns Promising Researcher award. Two awards are reserved for ALER members who make substantial contributions to the field and the organization: the Albert J. Mazurkiewicz award and a Laureate award. ALER also supports a literacy-related project (the Judy Richardson Literacy as a Living Legacy award) and research that supports literacy teacher education (the Literacy Teacher Education award).

ALER's committee and commission structure affords leadership opportunities while also supporting the mission and operations of the association. These committees and commissions include Membership, Elections, Professional Affairs, Program, Publications, Resolution and Rules, Awards, Public Information, Webmaster, Legislative and Governmental Affairs, Research, and Reading Room/Exhibits.

Opportunities to collaborate and receive professional support and encouragement abound—whether jointly planning for a conference proposal, interacting with other volunteers who hold committee or commission membership, serving on editorial boards, working within the various projects pursued by the four divisions, or attending mentoring sessions offered at the annual conference. ALER collaborates with other associations such as the International Reading Association (IRA) and the National Council for the Accreditation of Teacher Education (NCATE) through jointly sponsored conference sessions. ALER mentors members through establishing bonds between new members and established leaders in the field. For more information, visit the ALER website at http://www.aleronline.org.

International Reading Association

Victoria Risko, President, 2011–2012 The International Reading Association (IRA) is a nonprofit organization committed to promoting literacy around the world. For its more than 60,000 members, the IRA supports literacy leaders with multiple resources. Literacy leaders, as IRA members, include classroom teachers, reading specialists, literacy coaches, teaching and curriculum specialists, literacy teacher educators, and literacy researchers. They have access to multiple publications and professional development forums and materials, and opportunities to serve on committees and collaborate with colleagues as members of special–interest groups. Each of these resources is described as follows:

- The IRA's website is http://reading.org. On the website, literacy leaders will find information about the IRA's mission, its governance, and its resources.
- Publications: http://www.reading.org/General/Publications.aspx
  1. Books and videos provide information and demonstrations on research-based teaching practices. http://www.reading.org/General/Publications/Books .aspx http://www.reading.org/General/Publications/Videos.aspx

2. Three journals are published: *The Reading Teacher* (primarily geared toward elementary teachers), *Journal of Adolescent and Adult Literacy*, and *Reading Research Quarterly* (leading literacy research journal). http://www.reading.org/General/Publications/Journals.aspx

3. *Reading Today* is a bimonthly magazine that provides news of the Association and information about educational policies and teaching practices. http://www.reading.org/General/Publications/blog/About_Reading_Today.aspx

4. *Reading Online* provides access to hundreds of articles published in the IRA journals. These can be accessed through author, title, keyword, and subject indexes. http://www.readingonline.org/

5. *E-books*—A selection of IRA books is available in e-book format. http://www.reading.org/General/Publications/e-books.aspx

▪ Professional development forums and materials

1. All publications described above support professional development programs.

2. Lesson Plans provided by http://readwritethink.org. New lessons appear each month and apply across the grades. Podcasts highlight books for children and adolescents. Resources are available for parents and after-school programs. http://www.reading.org/Resources/LessonPlans.aspx

3. Podcasts are available on multiple topics related to K–12 teaching. http://www.reading.org/General/Publications/Podcasts.aspx

4. Webinars are offered on timely assessment and instructional topics. http://www.reading.org/General/Publications/webinars-archive.aspx

5. The Annual Convention, held in the spring, brings 8,000 to 12,000 literacy leaders together to hear speakers, conduct and attend professional development seminars, and collaborate with colleagues. http://www.reading.org/convention.aspx

▪ Opportunities are available to join state and local councils or international and national affiliates, to serve on committees and collaborate with colleagues. The council and affiliate networks bring together literacy leaders in 60 countries. http://www.reading.org/General/LocalAssociations.aspx

▪ Committees and special-interest groups provide opportunities for leadership and professional development. http://www.reading.org/General/AdvocacyandOutreach.aspx

▪ Technological resources are offered primarily through the IRA (http://www.reading.org); this website provides weekly editions of *Reading Today Online* and access to blogs and professional book discussion groups through links to Facebook and Twitter.

▪ Advocacy services are available whereby the IRA offers webinars and legislative update materials on U.S. policies and governmental actions. Legislative workshops are held for literacy leaders to prepare them for addressing policy issues with legislators. http://www.reading.org/General/Legislative.aspx

Literacy Research Association

Patricia Anders, President The Literacy Research Association (LRA) supports literacy leaders by providing a community of scholars dedicated to promoting research that enriches the knowledge, understanding, and development of lifespan literacies in a multicultural and multilingual world. Literacy leaders are invited to attend, present, and participate in the annual conference, to publish in the journal, and to enjoy all other benefits of membership in the association.

Resources

The Association offers peer-reviewed research, member networking opportunities, a membership listserv, and opportunities to serve the literacy research community.

Website

The Literacy Research Association's website that includes a research repository for member use can be accessed at http://www.literacyresearchassociation.org.

Conference

The Association meets annually. For the past 50 years, the conference has been held the week after Thanksgiving. It is held at a location in the southern United States and rotates from the eastern to the central to the western parts of the country. Papers are proposed for presentation by both members and nonmembers, which then receive peer review and notification of acceptance or rejection. The conference features peer-reviewed research presentations in the form of round tables, paper sessions, alternative formats, and symposia. Plenary speeches include the presidential address, two talks by invited scholars not typically attending the conference, and an annual review of research presented by a member. The conference program also features study groups, committee meetings, receptions, and a luncheon for newcomers and graduate students. Members value the time and opportunity for small-group interaction. Publishers display and sell scholarly books and donate books to the "silent auction." The Conference Program and presentations are available online and may be accessed from the "Conference" tab on the Web page.

Publications

The Literacy Research Association (LRA) publishes a journal, yearbook, and "policy briefs." The *Journal of Literacy Research*, which is in most academic libraries, is published quarterly, and is a peer-reviewed journal. The LRA yearbook is a peer-reviewed publication of papers presented at the conference. It is a benefit of conference registration and is available in most academic libraries. Past yearbooks are currently being uploaded to the website. Policy briefs are written by LRA members and are intended to summarize research on a topic relevant to current policy issues.

Special-Interest Groups

The LRA identifies a group with common scholarly interests as an innovative community group (ICG). ICGs are initiated by members and report to the board of directors through a board-member liaison. Presently, ICGs include the following: Doctoral Student ICG, History ICG, International ICG, and Multilingual/ Transcultural Literacies ICG.

Committees

The LRA is governed by an elected board of directors and committees made up of appointed members. The following committees play a critical role in the governance of the association: Technology; Research; Publications; Policy and Legislative; Field Council; Ethnicity, Race, and Multilingualism; Ethics; and seven award committees.

National Council of Teachers of English

Yvonne Siu-Runyan, Immediate Past President The National Council of Teachers of English (NCTE) is devoted *and* committed to improving the teaching and learning of English and the language arts at all levels of education. This is how the NCTE framed its mission in 1990 (http://www .ncte.org/mission):

> The Council promotes the development of literacy, the use of language to construct personal and public worlds and to achieve full participation in society, through the learning and teaching of English and the related arts and sciences of language.

Here is a summary of the remarkable resources that NCTE has developed for its members, including online professional development services, professional books and journals, an annual convention, and meetings of affiliates and constituent groups throughout the country.

NCTE's *New* National Center for Literacy Education: http://www.ncleliteracy.org

After decades of top-down reforms and interventions from those far away from the classroom, the NCTE decided that something had to be done to empower teachers to share, collaborate, and learn together for the sake of our young, our profession, and our country.

Rather than bashing schools and teachers, the NCTE and the Ball Foundation (http://www.ballfoundation.org/) decided to build the National Center for Literacy Education (NCLE). The NCLE compiles evidence about how educators working in cross-disciplinary teams design and implement plans to support literacy learners in every classroom. By "telling our stories"—vignettes and case studies from these schools—the NCLE is not only making visible teaching and learning practices, but also highlighting the conditions that make authentic and meaningful learning possible.

Conventions

The NCTE hosts an annual convention each November (http://www.ncte.org/annual), and constituent organizations meet regularly as well. Many state affiliates also hold annual meetings.

In my presidential address at the 2011 NCTE Annual Convention in Chicago, I encouraged each of you to tell *your* stories because doing so makes facts come alive. Most noneducators do not know the ins and outs of our job and how we nurture and worry about their children. By telling our stories, we are collectively telling the truth.

Pathways: http://www.ncte.org/pathways

Pathways is an online resource for teacher-learning communities committed to continuous improvement in both student learning and teacher knowledge. I invite you to take a tour at http://www.ncte.org/pathways/tour; you will see teachers in action. Please contact the NCTE at pathways@ncte.org for more information.

Anti-Censorship Resources: http://www.ncte.org/action/anti-censorship

The Anti-Censorship Center offers resources for teachers and others facing censorship challenges. The website offers information on how to report a censorship incident or get advice on dealing with a book or film challenge.

Publications

The NCTE publishes 10 peer-reviewed journals (http://www.ncte.org/journals) offering the latest in research, classroom examples and lessons, and novel ideas for educators at all levels. *Language Arts* and *Voices from the Middle* also offer podcasts (http://www.ncte.org/journals/la/podcasts and http://www.ncte.org/journals/vm/podcasts).

In addition to *reading* NCTE publications, I encourage you to *write* for the Council; visit http://www.ncte.org/write/journals for more information.

The NCTE also cosponsors ReadWriteThink (http://www.readwritethink.org), which offers free lesson plans written by teachers, as well as classroom resources, professional development opportunities, and parent and after-school resources. Learn about writing or reviewing for ReadWriteThink at http://www.readwritethink.org/util/contribute-to-rwt.html.

And don't forget the NCTE's books! There is something for everyone in the wealth of titles in the NCTE's online store: https://secure.ncte.org/store/. New titles include a series of grade-leveled books (Pre-K–2, 3–5, 6–8, and 9–12) designed to help teachers navigate the Common Core State Standards while adhering to the NCTE's philosophy and principles of effective teaching: https://secure.ncte.org/store/commoncorestandards/publications.

Awards, Awards, Awards: http://www.ncte.org/awards

To recognize those who have contributed greatly to the Council, the NCTE has established many awards honoring teaching, writing, research, service, and more. For a complete list of awards, visit http://www.ncte.org/awards/alphaawardslist.

National Day on Writing: http://www.ncte.org/dayonwriting

In 2009, at the request of the NCTE, the U.S. Senate passed a Resolution declaring October 20th as the National Day on Writing. A free digital archive of more than 30,000 pieces of writing—including short stories, essays, videos, blog entries, artwork, and text messages—can be found at http://www.galleryofwriting.org. To contribute writing, visit http://www.galleryofwriting.org/contribute.php. You can even start your own gallery: http://www.galleryofwriting.org/gallery_start.php.

The NCTE has also put together some tips to keep in mind as you and your students write: http://www.ncte.org/dayonwriting/tips.

Online Conversations: http://ncte.connectedcommunity.org/NCTE/Home

I love the NCTE Connected Community, an online discussion space where teachers share their lessons and what they learned, or discuss heavy items, such as how to teach text structure. I also enjoy the pointed questions they ask, for they provide alternate views and make me question what I think I know.

For additional online interaction, you can become a fan of the NCTE on Facebook (http://www.facebook.com/ncte.org) and follow the NCTE on Twitter (http://twitter.com/ncte).

NCTE: A Work in Progress

The NCTE, a vibrant, professional organization, will always be a work in progress. Only time will tell what the future holds for the Council, but I can emphatically say that NCTE has mattered for teachers, students, parents, and the general public for 100 years.

Through good times and hard times, the NCTE has prevailed because of excellent fiscal management; the generosity of and sacrifices made by staff, the presidents, and members; as well a commitment to listening to our members' concerns and acting on their behalf—hallmarks of a healthy organization.

Afterword

As reflective literacy leaders, we believe it is important to consider, articulate, and share our intentions beyond this book and encourage our readers to do the same. What is next for us? What will happen to all of the ideas we hold about literacy leadership within the pages of this text? What are our next intentions?

Cindy will continue as a college professor teaching undergraduates and graduates to develop their literacy-leadership skills. Also, she will explore the possibilities for reaching out to educators to extend her own and others' understandings about literacy leadership through focused research, publications, and workshop presentations. She plans to stay actively involved in New York State educational policy development as new issues develop. She would love to hear from you at cindy.lassonde@oneonta.edu.

Kristine will continue literacy-leadership work as a seventh-grade writing teacher. Within the context of her classroom space, she plans to further explore transformative learning and how appreciative leadership/appreciative coaching can be used to enhance learning. In addition, Kristine is creating a writing curriculum in service of a larger mission and vision: teaching humane education—environmental ethics, animal protection, human rights, culture and change—in ways that resonate with the key themes of literacy leadership as found on these pages. She would love to hear from you and to collaborate on the occasion these interests match yours. She can be reached at ktucker1972@yahoo.com.

And so, we ask—what are your next intentions beyond this book?

Index

accountability, 4, 54, 117–119

adequate yearly progress, 5, 14

administrators, xvii, xxiii, xxv, 4, 11, 16–17, 24, 27, 32, 40, 46, 49, 52–54, 61, 68, 75–76, 83, 85, 87–88, 92, 96, 132

adult learners,
   assumptions about, 68–76
   working with, 65

American Reading Company, 14, 124, 151

American Reading Forum, 14, 18, 124, 153–154

assessment
   changes in, 5
   expectations, 4
   of literacy leadership, 114, 139–141, 146, 148
   of progress, 55, 139–141
   of professional learning, 5
   of students, 5, 7, 9, 59, 78
   RTI, 11
   situated, 55
   standardized, 26, 50–54

Association of Literacy Educators and Researchers, 14, 17, 124, 154

appreciative coaching, 21, 32–35, 37, 42, 121, 161

best practices, 40, 95, 96, 120

case scenarios, 49, 50–51, 53, 55, 58, 71–76, 80, 102

celebrating successes, 142, 145–146

Classroom Activities, 18, 42, 60, 81, 102, 121, 137, 149

coaching, 22, 57–58, 89–91, 101, 109, 110, 119, 141
   appreciative, 21, 32–37, 42, 121, 161
   creative, 105
   Literacy Coaching Clearinghouse, 127
   resources for, 151, 153

collaboration, xxi, xxiii, xxiv, 6, 15, 22–23, 25–26, 28–30, 34, 40–41, 54, 56, 59, 114, 121, 127, 131–132
   benefits of, 146
   collaborative professional development models, 132
   opportunities for, 153
   partnerships, 131–132

Common Core State Standards (CCSS), xxi, xxv, 5, 36, 41, 49, 50, 54, 78, 89, 100–101, 108, 110, 114, 120, 140, 153

Common Core State Standards Connection, 5, 6, 23–24, 49, 50, 65, 66, 85, 86, 108, 109, 125, 126, 140, 141
   navigating, 160
   Text Complexity Strands, 152

communication
   artful, 83–85
   as a process, 89–93, 96
   collaborative, 88–89
   critical, 85, 100–101
   discussions
      large-group, 94–95
      small-group and individual, 95–96
   proactive, 85
   providing feedback, 7, 22, 28, 56, 83, 84, 86, 87, 101–103, 112, 137,
   the listener, 92–93
   the speaker, 89–92
   intent, 93
   written, 96–97

connected literacy leader, 130

creativity, 40, 66, 107–110, 115, 117, 120, 121, 123, 133, 135

Critical Voices, xxv, 8, 13, 16, 37, 40, 45, 48, 56, 56, 58, 70, 78–79, 98, 100, 115, 117, 133, 135, 145, 147

culture, 34, 113, 161
   inquiry, 113
   literacy leadership, 8, 14–15, 17, 27–29, 34
   popular, 102
   professional development, 5, 70
   school, xxiii, 7, 9, 23, 31, 46, 48, 76, 87, 131, 146
   transforming the, 7, 54, 77, 108, 120

curriculum, 5, 7–9, 13, 16, 22, 42, 47, 50–51, 95, 100, 105, 116, 118–120, 131–132135, 140, 155
   core, 117
   design, 117
   framework, 113

curriculum-based measurement (CBM), 11, 67

efficacy, 33, 54, 67
empowerment, 26, 60, 75,
engaging in learning, 68
ethics
    committees, 13, 57, 158
    environmental, 161
    ethical approaches, 15, 38, 80, 90, 98, 102,
    literacy communities, 12, 57–58
    responsibility, 14
    The Ethical Literacy Leader, xxiv, 7, 12–15, 37–39,
        45, 54, 56–58, 71, 77–79, 98–100, 115–116,
        133, 142, 145
    values, 116
evidence-based literacy pedagogy, 47
experience, xxiv, 26–37, 39, 40

family, 11, 18, 46–50, 84
    literacy, 154

goals for literacy leaders, xxiii, 5, 37, 45–48, 49, 54,
        56, 58–59, 61, 66–67, 89, 91, 140–141
    resetting, 141

improving student performance, 47
individual approach to literacy leadership, 9, 10
interdisciplinary team, 14–15
internal needs, 174
International Reading Association, xix, 13, 14, 15, 16,
        38, 56, 57, 123, 124, 132, 142, 154–156

literacy communities, xxiii, 13, 25–26, 54, 65, 68, 139
    as levers for change, 12
    collaborative, 60
    effectiveness of, 140
    literacy-learning communities, 54–56, 83, 145
    progress of, 139
    transformative, 137
Literacy Research Association, xv, 124, 157–158

narrative inquiry, 21, 26–28, 32–34, 37, 42, 109
National Council of Teachers of English, xix, 124,
        127, 158–160
networking, 31, 56, 123, 125, 127, 136, 157
    social, 129
No Child Left Behind, xxi, xxiii, 4, 49, 77

Partnership for Assessment of Readiness for College
        and Careers (PARCC), 139
partnerships (see collaboration)
professional development, 7, 16, 23, 24, 45, 50–52,
        58–61, 76–77, 94, 117, 119, 123, 131

effect of No Child Left Behind on, 4
effective, 49, 53–56, 65, 67–71, 87
efforts, 5, 9, 28–29, 40, 151, 155
grants and funding for, 41, 75
ongoing, 5
organizing, 47, 111–114
online, 125, 127, 128, 136, 158
Professional Development Activities, 18, 22, 42, 49,
        60, 81, 102, 121, 137, 149
    resources for, 156, 159
    school-wide, 5
professional literacy associations, 123–124
professional standards, 13, 45–46, 54, 57–58

Race to the Top, xxi, xxiii, 5, 148
Reading First, 19
reform, 6, 19, 38–39, 55, 56
    education, xxiii
    teacher-evaluation, 5
    top-down, 158
    whole-school, 9, 125, 151
relationships, 55, 59–60, 68–70, 77, 79, 84–85, 87,
        106, 111, 113, 131, 132, 136
resistance, 28, 58–60, 89, 93, 119, 135
Response to Intervention (RTI), xv, xxi, xxv, 9, 78,
        110, 116
Response to Intervention (RTI) and the Literacy
        Leader, 11, 21–22, 45–46, 65, 67, 96–97,
        106, 125, 142–143
Ridge and Valley Charter School, xxv,
        110–115, 120
role of literacy leaders, xxiv, 21, 27, 31, 71, 73, 79,
        131, 134
    defining, 24, 28
    in a literacy-learning community, 55–59
    redefining, xxiii, 4, 8–13, 16–17, 144, 148

school mission, 113, 120
stakeholders, 5, 8, 11–12, 16–17, 22, 38–39, 75, 133
    collaborating with, 131–136
student achievement, 4, 5, 26, 49, 140, 141
systems thinking, 7, 21–23, 25–26, 32–34, 37, 39, 42,
        109, 114

teacher evaluation, 139
    reform, 5
team approach to literacy leadership, 9–11
types of literacy leadership
    diffused, 10
    flattened, 10
    Lone-Ranger, 10

Photo Credits

Photo Credits

Brent Alexander Frohmader: Photographic campus icon, Jana Lichtenberg icon, word
push button, Jan Wall Detweiler word bank icon, Scout illustration. Orelia Bird: bird
pattern, Robert Pickett, page 9, top; Cindy Kassab: page 14 bottom; Kennan C.
Jackson: page 2; Stefan Sokolowski: page 20; Janet Wall Frohmader: page 24; Janet Wall
Frohmader: page 64; Tim Crawford: page 84; Roy Morsch Photolibra: page 104; Janet
Wall Frohmader: page 122; Lucian Milasan Photolibra: page 138; (background) Stefan